*From the Kitchen of:*

_____

_____

_____

# THE
# VeganEgg™
## Cookbook

# THE
# VÉGANEGG™
## *Cookbook*

**A Collection of Delicious and Creative
Recipes Made With VeganEgg**

Recipes Curated by Jenny Engel and Heather Bell of Spork Foods®
Photography by Oscar Mendoza, Chris Petrellese and Jasmine Briones

Published in United States by Follow Your Heart
www.followyourheart.com

"Follow Your Heart", "Vegenaise", "VeganEgg" are registered trademarks of Old Friends Holdings, LLC
"Earth Island" is a registered trademark of Earth Island

Designed by Sara Farwell and Cristine Kasha
Cover photo provided by Chris Petrellese and Jasmine Briones
Animal photos provided by Farm Sanctuary and Woodstock Farm Sanctuary
Additional recipe photos provided by Spork Foods, Eat.Drink.Shrink, Thug Kitchen

ISBN: 978-0-9721892-2-4

FIRST EDITION

10 9 8 7 6 5 4 3 2 1

# Table of Contents

Foreword by Colleen Holland ................................... 01

Introduction by Spork Foods ................................... 03

Kitchen Staples ................................................. 04

Tips for Working with VeganEgg ............................ 07

Early Eats ....................................................... 09

Delicious Dishes .............................................. 49

Tasty Treats ................................................... 83

Farm Sanctuaries ............................................. 115

Following Our Hearts ........................................ 119

40 Years of Flavor ........................................... 123

A VeganEgg is Hatched ...................................... 125

Why Plant-Based .............................................. 129

Contributors ................................................... 131

Acknowledgements ........................................... 135

Index ............................................................ 139

# Foreword

BY COLLEEN HOLLAND

**As the publisher of a vegan lifestyle magazine,** I have the unique privilege of trying all the latest plant-based products to hit the market. Some are good, others are great, and then there are those once-in-a-blue-moon products that knock it out of the ballpark. For me, VeganEgg lands squarely in the third category.

At VegNews, our team eagerly awaited VeganEgg's arrival, buzzing with excitement at the prospect of whipping up our first cruelty-free omelette—one without the cholesterol, fat, antibiotics, or pesticides found in its chicken-egg counterparts.

Straight off the bat, we were blown away by how easy it was to use, then, by how similar the consistency was to an actual chicken's egg. The ultimate test, though, was how it would taste. One bite of that first omelette—savory, fluffy, and remarkably "eggy"—and I knew I was experiencing something that could change the way America eats, and possibly save 300 million animal lives each year in the process.

An omelette like the one we made (and quickly devoured) is but one of a thousand uses for VeganEgg. It also scrambles, rises, and binds just like the animal version, which opens up an entire edible universe. In the forthcoming pages, you'll learn how to create mouthwatering waffles, quiches, pastas, meatballs, doughnuts, custards, and more from some of today's most talented plant-based chefs. These experts have perfected more than 30 recipes, so all you have to do is pick up VeganEgg and start cooking. Doing what's right for your health, the animals, and the planet has never been easier.

I am deeply grateful to the brilliant team at Follow Your Heart for making veganism such an accessible lifestyle to so many of us. Since 1970, this trendsetting company has helped shape the plant-based food landscape with such innovative products as Vegenaise, Dairy-Free Parmesan, Vegan Gourmet Sour Cream, and, now, VeganEgg. There is a reason my team and I named Follow Your Heart "VegNews' Company of the Year" in 2016, and I have no doubt we'll be seeing many more revolutionary products from them for years to come.

Tonight, I'll be making the Quiche Florentine, Vanilla Bean Custard, and Soft-Batch Chocolate Chip Cookies to share at our next staff meeting. How about you? With this book, the culinary exploration is guaranteed to be delicious—and with VeganEgg, the possibilities are limitless.

Happy cooking!

*Sincerely,*
*Colleen Holland*
*Publisher + Co-Founder VegNews Magazine*

# Introduction
## BY SPORK FOODS

**There is magic in the idea that when you** follow your heart, you end up exactly where you're supposed to be. We can vividly remember a time when our long summer days growing up in SoCal were filled with delicious trips to the original Follow Your Heart Market & Café. Since our early days of becoming vegan, Vegenaise has been a staple in our kitchen and the passion and love that comes with all their products has been inspirational to us as sisters, vegans, and environmentalists.

We take this moment now to reflect on the ten-plus-years since Spork Foods began. We started teaching vegan cooking classes out of our desire to show people how to cook meals that will connect, heal, and energize. The feedback that comes from our students on their success and increased confidence in the kitchen continues to inspire us to keep following our hearts and developing more amazing recipes to keep this food movement marching forward.

We believe that eating and cooking is a personal journey. The inspiration and dedication that owners Bob and Paul (and the entire FYH crew) have put into their products reflect our own pursuit in positively representing plant-based living and its appeal to folks of every food perspective. If we can help show that

vegan food is every bit as exciting, delicious, filling, nutritious, fancy, simple, and altogether satisfying, then we've done our job.

As we see our own families grow, our dream of building Spork Foods is now entering a new phase, expanding into the Follow Your Heart family as their brand ambassadors. When Follow Your Heart asked us to join forces on this cookbook to help develop and curate VeganEgg recipes, we were thrilled! It's been fun to see the inspiring recipes that so many fantastic chefs who share our passion came up with. We consider many of these contributors close friends and we are grateful for their ingenuity, passion, and enthusiasm for all things plant-based. This cookbook is just an introduction to the many ways VeganEgg can revolutionize vegan cooking. This is truly just the beginning. We invite and encourage you to get creative in your own kitchens and report back on your breakfast, lunch, dinner, and dessert table wins.

Now get cookin'!

*Sincerely,*
*Jenny + Heather*

# Kitchen Staples

## Neutral-Tasting Oil (Safflower)

Did you know that different oils have different heat points? Many of the recipes in this book cook VeganEgg using medium to high heat so we recommend a neutral-tasting oil like safflower which can withstand higher cooking temps.

## Sea Salt

While table salt and sea salt are each sodium chloride, they are sourced in different ways. We prefer sea salt as it comes directly from the sea and, unlike typical table salt, isn't processed to remove the trace minerals.

## Ground Black Pepper

Whether you like to grind your pepper fresh or have some in your pantry pre-ground, this ingredient is a VeganEgg must-have.

## Vegan Butter

Soy-free. Organic. Cultured. We promise there's a vegan butter out there just for you. We prefer the vegan butter sticks for easier measuring. We always make sure we've got some on hand and ready to go.

### Evaporated Cane Sugar

Less refined than typical table sugar, evaporated cane sugar maintains some of the natural golden hue of the sugar cane sap and has added benefits of using less energy and resources to produce. And, if available, choose organic and fair-trade for an even more sustainable option.

### Unsweetened Almond, Soy, or Cashew Milk

Non-dairy milk has come a long way and with so many options out there, the choice is yours. Just make sure it's ice-cold and your VeganEggs will come out great every time!

# Tips for Working with VeganEgg

**Measuring VeganEgg**

We recommend scooping VeganEgg from the bag but not packing it down into your measuring spoon or cup. One "egg" is a loosely filled measure that has been leveled off. This will help you get the most VeganEggs from your carton.

**Mixing VeganEgg**

Whisk until the clumps are gone and the VeganEgg mixture is smooth and slightly thickened. You can also use a blender for fluffier "eggs."

When replacing traditional eggs with VeganEgg, if the recipe calls for more than 2 eggs, we recommend reducing the water you mix with the VeganEgg powder by 25% (e.g. 6 tablespoons of water per VeganEgg). VeganEgg powder mixed with water contains more liquid than a traditional egg, which is why we cook it for a longer time.

**Baking with VeganEgg**

If you're baking with VeganEgg, you may need less water in your recipe. We recommend that if the recipe uses 1-2 eggs, use 5 tablespoons ice-cold water per VeganEgg. If the recipe uses 3+ eggs, use ¼ cup ice-cold water per VeganEgg. (These are general baking guidelines and individual recipes may vary.) If you're baking gluten-free, always use ¼ cup of ice-cold water per VeganEgg.

Be sure to use ice-cold water or non-dairy milk (less than 40°F). Place ice-cubes in a bowl with your water or non-dairy milk before you are ready to use it. You can also save the extra step and time by keeping some cold water in your fridge.

VeganEgg may be stored in your fridge or pantry. If stored in the fridge, keep your open bag of VeganEgg protected from moisture. After mixing VeganEgg powder with water or non-dairy milk, use immediately.

# EARLY
## *Eats*

### BREAKFAST *and* BRUNCH

The Perfect Scramble ............................................. 10

Chive & Cheese Scrambled VeganEggs ........................... 14

Pecan Waffles ................................................... 16

Breakfast Frittata Pie .......................................... 18

Spinach, "Ham," & Provolone Cheese Strata ...................... 22

Chipotle Breakfast Burrito ...................................... 26

Quiche Florentine ............................................... 28

Classic French Toast ............................................ 30

Rancho Chilaquiles .............................................. 32

Pumpkin French Toast Casserole .................................. 36

"Sausage" & VeganEgg Biscuit Sandwich ........................... 40

Breakfast Tacos with Creamy Tomatillo Sauce ..................... 44

# The Perfect Scramble

## BY FOLLOW YOUR HEART

**SERVES:** 2-4  **DIFFICULTY:** Easy
**PREP TIME:** 5 Minutes  **COOK TIME:** 8 Minutes

### TOOLS YOU'LL NEED

The best place to start is the beginning. When we set out to create VeganEgg, our first goal was to create a product that not only worked as a baking replacement, but successfully scrambled like a traditional egg. Mastering the scrambled VeganEgg is a key step in many of the following recipes in this cookbook, so get cooking and master that perfect scramble! (Gluten-Free)

¼ cup VeganEgg powder

1 cup ice-cold water

½ teaspoon sea salt

¼ teaspoon ground black pepper

2 teaspoons neutral-tasting oil (safflower)

01  Whisk or blend VeganEgg powder and ice-cold water until uniform and slightly thickened, about 1 minute. Set aside. Ice-cold water is very important here so be sure it's cold (less than 50°F).

**\*Begin here for other recipes referencing The Perfect Scramble**

02  Heat a lightly-oiled pan to medium-high. You want the pan already heated when you add the VeganEgg mixture. The size of your pan should correspond to the amount of VeganEgg you are cooking: 1-2 eggs works in a small-medium pan, but anything more, you will want a large enough pan to help the egg spread and cook evenly.

03  Pour VeganEgg mixture into pan ("egg" should sizzle and bubble) and start to scrape the mixture from the edge of the pan to the center, forming large soft curds.

04  Continue to scramble frequently and evenly with a spatula until eggs are firm. Take care to not overmix – the VeganEgg will need some time

*(Directions continued on next page)*

*(Continued from previous page)*

between scrambling to set up. You may need to reduce the heat of your pan if you see the egg start to brown. VeganEgg takes longer than regular eggs, so we recommend 6-8 minutes until fully cooked (at least 165°F). You will start to see the pieces of cooked VeganEgg start to look dry and the shine will fade away. Season to taste with salt and pepper and enjoy!

**Note:** If your VeganEgg scramble didn't quite set up, looks too liquid-y or goopy, make sure you didn't over agitate while cooking or use less than ice-cold water.

# Chive & Cheese Scrambled VeganEggs

## BY SPORK FOODS

**SERVES:** 2-4  **DIFFICULTY:** Easy
**PREP TIME:** 5 Minutes  **COOK TIME:** 8 Minutes

### TOOLS YOU'LL NEED

**Here's a refreshing take on the traditional scramble that's highlighted by the brightness of fresh lemon juice and the creaminess of our melted Provolone. Simple and elegantly satisfying! (Gluten-Free)**

¼ cup VeganEgg powder

1 cup ice-cold water

½ teaspoon sea salt

¼ teaspoon lemon pepper

2 teaspoons neutral-tasting oil (safflower)

2 teaspoons fresh lemon juice

2 tablespoons fresh chives, finely chopped

2 slices Follow Your Heart Provolone cheese, diced

01  To a mixing bowl, add VeganEgg powder, ice-cold water, sea salt, and lemon pepper. Whisk until uniform and slightly thickened, about 1 minute. Set aside.

02  Follow cooking directions for The Perfect Scramble (Page 10).

03  Stir in lemon juice, chives, Provolone cheese and cook 1 additional minute. Remove from heat and serve warm.

## Try These Other Variations:

• Sun-Dried Tomato, Chopped Basil and Mozzarella Cheese
• Pico de Gallo Salsa, Pepper Jack Cheese, and Sliced Avocado
• Sautéed Broccoli Pieces, Cheddar Cheese, and Black Pepper

# Pecan Waffles

BY ACOOBA SCOTT @acoobascott

**YIELDS:** 8 Large Waffles  **DIFFICULTY:** Easy
**PREP TIME:** 5-10 Minutes  **COOK TIME:** 4-5 Minutes per Waffle

## TOOLS YOU'LL NEED

Dust off that waffle iron and whip up these hearty pecan waffles. We love to drizzle them with real maple syrup and fresh berries or you can get adventurous with some caramelized peaches and sprigs of fresh basil. Let your imagination for toppings go wild!

1 cup unbleached all-purpose flour

1 cup whole wheat pastry flour

2 teaspoons baking powder

1 teaspoon baking soda

¼ cup evaporated cane sugar

1 teaspoon sea salt

3 tablespoons VeganEgg powder

¾ cup ice-cold water

1 tablespoon apple cider vinegar

1 ¾ cups unsweetened soy or almond milk

½ cup vegan butter, melted or neutral-tasting oil (safflower)

¾ cup pecans, finely chopped

01  Pre-heat waffle iron.

02  In a medium mixing bowl, add all-purpose flour, pastry flour, baking powder, baking soda, sugar and sea salt together and set aside.

03  To a large mixing bowl, add VeganEgg powder and ice-cold water. Whisk until uniform and slightly thickened, about 1 minute. Set aside.

04  In a large glass measuring cup, whisk apple cider vinegar into soymilk to curdle, and set aside, about 1-2 minutes.

05  Add curdled soymilk mixture and melted vegan butter or vegetable oil to VeganEgg mixture, and whisk until completely uniform.

06  Whisk dry ingredients into VeganEgg mixture, just until combined. Gently stir in pecans.

07  On a lightly greased, preheated waffle iron, cook about ⅓ cup batter at a time according to waffle iron directions, on a medium setting (setting 4). Serve warm with desired sweet or savory toppings.

# Breakfast Frittata Pie

## BY CAROLYN SCOTT-HAMILTON @healthyvoyager

**SERVES:** 4-6  **DIFFICULTY:** Moderate to Advanced
**PREP TIME:** 20 Minutes  **COOK TIME:** 40 Minutes

### TOOLS YOU'LL NEED

Who says that pie is only for dessert? The Healthy Voyager's Breakfast Frittata Pie is a savory and filling way to start your day. With crispy hash browns as the crust and some hearty veggies mixed with VeganEgg, this pie is a satisfying breakfast. Add a side of fresh fruit and you've got a complete meal for you and your family.
(Gluten-Free *be sure to check the vegan bacon bits' ingredients)

---

2 tablespoons neutral-tasting oil (safflower), divided

2 cups shredded hash brown potatoes, thawed

1 cup brown onion, diced, divided

½ cup Follow Your Heart Mozzarella Shreds

2 garlic cloves, minced

1 cup fresh cremini mushrooms, thinly sliced

1 cup fresh tomato, diced

3 cups fresh baby spinach, packed

½ cup VeganEgg powder

2 cups ice-cold water

¼ cup unsweetened almond, soy or cashew milk

½ teaspoon sea salt

¼ teaspoon ground black pepper

¼ cup vegan bacon bits, for topping

01  Preheat oven to 375°F. Grease a 9-inch pie plate with cooking spray.

02  In sauté pan, add 1 tablespoon oil and sauté hash browns with ½ cup diced onions until well incorporated, and onions are softened, 6-8 minutes.

03  Press down hash brown and onion mix into greased pie plate. Bake for about 10 minutes, or until crisp. Remove from oven and top with Follow Your Heart Mozzarella Shreds. Set aside.

04  Heat remaining tablespoon of oil in a skillet over medium heat and add garlic, remaining ½ cup diced onions, mushrooms and diced tomato. Cook for about 3 minutes, stirring frequently. Add spinach and cook about 2 more minutes. Remove from heat and spread sautéed vegetable mix over cheese.

05  In a mixing bowl, whisk VeganEgg powder and ice-cold water until smooth and slightly thickened, about 1 minute. Add almond, soy or

*(Directions continued on next page)*

*(Continued from previous page)*

cashew milk, sea salt and pepper and whisk until thoroughly combined.

06 Pour VeganEgg mixture over all ingredients, until covered and to the rim. Top with vegan bacon bits. Bake for about 30 minutes, or until top is golden brown. Let cool for 10 minutes before cutting and enjoy!

# Spinach, "Ham," & Provolone Cheese Strata

## BY CHEF ROBIN SWALLOW @robinswallow

**SERVES:** 6-8   **DIFFICULTY:** Advanced
**PREP TIME:** 30 Minutes + Chilling Time   **COOK TIME:** 85-95 Minutes

### TOOLS YOU'LL NEED

**Save precious weekend sleep-in time by prepping this breakfast strata the night before and simply baking it in the morning. This family-style recipe is great for serving a big family brunch and travels well if you're heading to a breakfast pot luck. (Gluten-Free if you use gluten-free bread, such as Follow Your Heart Brioche)**

¼ cup vegan butter

1 ½ cups brown onion, finely chopped

10 slices vegan ham, diced

1 teaspoon sea salt, divided

½ teaspoon ground black pepper, divided

Dash freshly grated nutmeg

2 (10 oz.) packages frozen chopped spinach, thawed and drained

8 cups French or Italian bread, cut into 1-inch cubes

1 ½ cups grated Follow Your Heart Provolone Cheese

½ cup grated Follow Your Heart Parmesan cheese

2 ½ cups ice-cold water

2 cups ice-cold unsweetened almond or soy milk

1 cup, plus 2 tablespoons VeganEgg powder

01   Grease a 3-quart baking dish.

02   Melt vegan butter in a medium skillet over medium heat. Add onions to pan and sauté until soft, about 5 minutes. Add diced ham, ½ teaspoon salt, ¼ teaspoon black pepper, and nutmeg. Continue to cook for 1 minute more. Stir in spinach, remove from the heat and set aside.

03   Layer bottom of greased baking dish with one third of the bread cubes. Top with one third of spinach and ham mixture and one third of each of the cheeses. Repeat these layers twice more with the bread, spinach and cheese.

04   Add ice-cold water and milk to blender. Add VeganEgg powder, remaining ½ teaspoon salt and ¼ teaspoon black pepper. Mix until blended and uniform. Pour VeganEgg mixture evenly over bread and spinach layered in baking dish. Cover with plastic wrap and chill for at least 8 hours and no longer than 12 hours.

*(Directions continued on next page)*

*(Continued from previous page)*

05  Remove from refrigerator 30 minutes before
    baking. Preheat oven to 350˚F. Bake uncovered
    until puffed, golden brown and cooked through,
    45-55 minutes. Let stand at least 5 minutes
    before serving and enjoy!

# Chipotle Breakfast Burrito

## BY FOLLOW YOUR HEART

**YIELDS:** 4 Burritos   **DIFFICULTY:** Easy
**PREP TIME:** 5 Minutes   **COOK TIME:** 15-20 Minutes

### TOOLS YOU'LL NEED

A breakfast burrito could be our breakfast every. single. day. Once you've scrambled up the VeganEgg, the additions and variations are endless but our absolute favorite is this classic VeganEgg, black bean and Chipotle Vegenaise combo.
**(Gluten-Free if you use corn tortillas or Follow Your Heart Gluten-Free Tortillas)**

½ cup VeganEgg powder

2 cups ice-cold water

½ teaspoon sea salt

¼ teaspoon ground black pepper

2 teaspoons vegan butter

1 tablespoon neutral-tasting oil (safflower)

1 cup frozen hash browns

4 large flour tortillas or Follow Your
Heart Gluten-Free Tortillas

2 tablespoons Follow Your Heart
Chipotle Vegenaise

1 cup black beans, rinsed and drained

1 cup fresh pico de gallo

2 tablespoons fresh chives, finely chopped

01  To a mixing bowl, add VeganEgg powder, ice-cold water, sea salt, and black pepper. Set aside.

02  Follow cooking directions for The Perfect Scramble (Page 10).

03  Meanwhile, heat a separate non-stick skillet over medium heat. Add oil and frozen hash browns. Cook according to directions, or until crisp, about 5 minutes. Set aside.

04  Lay 4 tortillas on a work surface. Spread ½ tablespoon Chipotle Vegenaise into the center of each tortilla in a line. Add ¼ cup cooked hash browns, ¼ cup scrambled VeganEgg, ¼ cup black beans, ¼ cup pico de gallo, and ½ tablespoon chives to center of each tortilla in a line, leaving about 2 inches on the left and right sides of the tortilla for rolling.

05  To roll, fold left side of tortilla slightly over fillings, fold over right side to slightly cover fillings and fold bottom of tortilla over entire amount of fillings. Roll up and away from you, creating a burrito shape. Serve warm.

# Quiche Florentine

## BY FOLLOW YOUR HEART

**YIELDS:** 6-8 Slices   **DIFFICULTY:** Easy
**PREP TIME:** 15 Minutes   **COOK TIME:** 60-65 Minutes

### TOOLS YOU'LL NEED

This no-fuss, tasty recipe is a great way to sneak in some greens and brings an element of fancy to your table. Serve with some freshly-squeezed orange juice (and maybe a splash of champagne) and raise your pinky finger high!
(Gluten-Free with a gluten-free pie crust)

1- 9-inch frozen pie crust

1 tablespoon vegan butter

½ cup shallots, thinly sliced

6 tablespoons VeganEgg powder

1 ½ cups ice-cold water

¾ cup coconut creamer

pinch ground nutmeg

¾ teaspoon sea salt

⅛ teaspoon cayenne pepper

½ cup Follow Your Heart Provolone, shredded (or any FYH cheese of your choice)

1- 10 oz. package frozen chopped spinach, defrosted and wrung entirely free of water

01   Preheat oven to 400°F.

02   Thaw crust until just soft enough (about 10 minutes) to easily prick bottom and sides with fork. Bake crust on center rack until fully cooked and lightly golden, 10 minutes or as directed on package. If crust puffs up while cooking, gently prick with fork to deflate. Set aside and turn oven down to 325°F.

03   Heat vegan butter in a small sauté pan over medium-low heat. Cook shallots until soft and translucent, about 8 minutes. Do not brown. Set aside to cool.

04   In a medium bowl, measure VeganEgg powder, nutmeg, sea salt, and cayenne pepper. Add ice-cold water and whisk until smooth. Then pour in coconut creamer and whisk to incorporate.

05   Place cooked pie crust on a baking sheet. Evenly spread shallots, cheese, and spinach over bottom of cooked crust (breaking up clumps as best you can), then pour VeganEgg mixture on top.

06   Bake at 325°F for 50-55 minutes until custard is set and top is lightly golden. Serve hot or warm.

# *Classic French Toast*

## BY SPORK FOODS

**YIELDS:** 6-8 Slices   **DIFFICULTY:** Easy
**PREP TIME:** 5 Minutes   **COOK TIME:** 6 Minutes

### TOOLS YOU'LL NEED

This breakfast staple is simple and easy to make, but its flavor (and aroma) is luxurious. As the first slice begins to sizzle on the pan, your kitchen will be filled with the wonderful smell of cinnamon and vanilla. Smother each slice in maple syrup and fresh fruit and dig right in! (Gluten-Free with gluten-free bread)

¼ cup VeganEgg powder

1 cup ice-cold almond or soy milk

½ teaspoon sea salt

1 teaspoon ground cinnamon

½ teaspoon ground allspice

¼ teaspoon ground cardamom

3 tablespoons maple syrup

1 ½ teaspoon vanilla extract

2 tablespoons neutral-tasting oil (safflower), plus additional oil for coating pan

6-8 slices Follow Your Heart Gluten-Free Brioche or bread of your choice

01   In a medium bowl, whisk together VeganEgg powder, ice-cold almond or soy milk, sea salt, cinnamon, allspice, cardamom, maple syrup, vanilla extract, and oil. Whisk until smooth and slightly thickened, about 1 minute. Set aside.

02   Pre-heat griddle or pan to a medium-high heat. Grease griddle with additional oil.

03   Coat each slice of bread in batter letting excess drip back into bowl and then place on hot pan or griddle.

04   Cook until slightly golden, about 3 minutes. Flip and cook for about another 3 minutes, or until golden. Serve warm and top with real maple syrup and fresh fruit of your choice.

# Rancho Chilaquiles

## BY THUG KITCHEN

**SERVES:** 4-6 **DIFFICULTY:** Moderate
**PREP TIME:** 15-20 Minutes **COOK TIME:** 40-45 Minutes

### TOOLS YOU'LL NEED

*"Chilaquiles are just a breakfast taco salad. So start your day with a salad good enough to chila-kill your hangover." – THUG KITCHEN (Gluten-Free)*

**Rancho Sauce Ingredients (3 cups total)**

1 (15 oz) can diced, fire-roasted tomatoes

½ cup vegetable broth

1 cup fresh cilantro, chopped

1 small white onion, chopped

1 jalapeño or Serrano pepper, seeds removed

2 tablespoons mild chili powder blend

2 tablespoons fresh lime juice

½ teaspoon ground cumin

¼ teaspoon sea salt

8 corn tortillas or 3 big handfuls of left over corn chips

**VeganEgg Ingredients**

½ cup VeganEgg powder

2 cups ice-cold water

1 tablespoon Bragg's liquid aminos, soy sauce or tamari

1 teaspoon garlic powder

2 teaspoon olive oil

2 tablespoons nutritional yeast (nooch)

01 For the rancho sauce, throw canned tomatoes, broth, cilantro, onion, jalapeño, chili powder, lime juice, cumin, and sea salt all together in a blender or food processor and let that run until sauce looks pretty smooth. Set aside because we're gonna come back to that in a sec.

02 If you're using chips just bust those out and skip this step. Otherwise, warm your oven up to 400°F. Cut your tortillas up into 8 triangular slices, you know, like a pizza. Spread the slices out on a baking sheet and throw them in the oven for 15-20 minutes to dry out. Stir them around halfway through. It's fine if they start to get hard in some spots but don't let them burn. When they're all crispy set them aside and now you're in business.

03 Whisk or blend together VeganEgg powder, ice-cold water, Braggs, and garlic powder until everything is mixed up and there aren't any chunks. Heat up the oil over a medium heat in a large skillet. Pour in VeganEgg mixture and using a spatula start to scramble it up. Stir in nooch, and keep scrambling for about 5 minutes. It's

*(Ingredients & Directions continued on next page)*

**Remaining Ingredients**

1 teaspoon olive oil

½ medium onion, chopped

1 bell pepper, chopped

1 to 2 jalapeños, chopped

2 cloves of garlic, minced

3 cups fresh spinach

**Toppings**

avocado

cilantro

jalapeños

pico de gallo

gonna be a little undercooked but that's exactly what you're going for, so just trust us and put the egg on a plate and move on. Wipe the skillet down and throw it right back on the stove cause we ain't done yet.

04   Heat up the next teaspoon of oil over medium heat in that same skillet. Throw in the onion, bell pepper, and jalapeños and sauté until onion starts to look a little brown, about 5-7 minutes. Add garlic and spinach and cook for 30 more seconds. Add chips or crispy tortillas and 2 cups rancho sauce. Fold in VeganEgg and another ½ cup of rancho sauce and let this all simmer together for about 5-7 minutes so that tortillas soften up and spinach is all wilted. By this point everyone will probably be headed into the kitchen to see what smells so awesome but tell them to chill out and wash some dishes until it's ready.

05   When it's looking good to go, pour on remaining rancho sauce, and then turn off heat. Serve right away topped with sliced avocado, a sprinkle of cilantro, more jalapeños and salsa or hot sauce. Don't share until someone else promises to wash the dishes.

# Pumpkin French Toast Casserole

## BY GABRIELLE ST. CLAIRE @eat.drink.shrink

**SERVES:** 6-8  **DIFFICULTY:** Moderate to Advanced
**PREP TIME:** 30 Minutes + Chilling Time  **COOK TIME:** 1 Hour

### TOOLS YOU'LL NEED

**A little bit country and a little bit rock 'n roll, this luscious casserole is decadent like dessert though we choose to serve it for breakfast as a sweet and special treat. When we served this one in our offices, the casserole pan was practically licked clean.**

### VeganEgg Ingredients

5 tablespoons VeganEgg powder
2 ½ cups ice-cold unsweetened almond milk

### Casserole Ingredients

¾ cup almond milk
½ cup pumpkin puree
½ cup packed brown sugar
2 teaspoons pumpkin pie spice blend
1 teaspoon ground cinnamon
1 teaspoon vanilla extract
1 large loaf of bread, cubed

### Crumble Topping Ingredients

¼ cup unbleached all-purpose flour
¼ cup brown sugar, packed
½ teaspoon cinnamon
¼ cup vegan butter, cut into cubes
¼ cup, plus ½ cup pecans roughly chopped

01  Lightly grease a 9 x 13 baking dish.

02  In a bowl, add VeganEgg powder with ice-cold almond milk. Whisk until smooth and slightly thickened, about 1 minute.

03  In large mixing bowl, whisk together almond milk, pumpkin puree, sugar, pumpkin pie spice, cinnamon, and vanilla extract.

04  Place a layer of bread cubes evenly into baking dish.

05  Combine pumpkin mixture with VeganEgg mixture and pour evenly over top leaving a few bread cubes uncoated. Store covered overnight in refrigerator, at least 8 hours and no more than 12 hours.

06  Remove from refrigerator 20 minutes before baking. Preheat oven to 350°F. Bake for 10-15 minutes.

07  While baking, make crumble by combining flour, brown sugar, cinnamon, vegan butter, ¼ cup pecans and confectioners' sugar until uniform and until mixture resembles coarse crumbs.

*(Ingredients & Directions continued on next page)*

*(Continued from previous page)*

2 tablespoons confectioners' sugar, plus for topping if desired

08  Remove casserole from oven and sprinkle the crumb topping evenly over top, along with remaining ½ cup pecans.

09  Place back into oven and bake for 35-45 minutes, or until golden brown. Serve immediately, sprinkled with additional confectioners' sugar, if desired.

# "Sausage" & VeganEgg Biscuit Sandwich

## BY SPORK FOODS

**SERVES:** 4-6 **DIFFICULTY:** Moderate
**PREP TIME:** 15 Minutes **COOK TIME:** 30 Minutes

## TOOLS YOU'LL NEED

**What better way to serve up VeganEgg than on a freshly made biscuit? The VeganEgg in this recipe is cooked slightly different than the scramble by letting it set up and then flipping it, similar to an omelet. With the folded VeganEgg, this sandwich is an easy and perfect on-the-go treat.**

### Biscuit Ingredients

1 ¼ cups unbleached all-purpose flour

2 teaspoons evaporated cane sugar

2 teaspoons ground golden flax seeds

½ teaspoon sea salt

¼ teaspoon ground black pepper

¼ teaspoon garlic powder

½ teaspoon dried basil

1 ½ teaspoons non-aluminum baking powder

¼ cup vegan butter

½ cup, plus 1 tablespoon unsweetened almond or soy milk

1 tablespoon maple syrup

### Remaining Ingredients

6 level tablespoons VeganEgg powder

1 ½ cups ice-cold water

½ teaspoon sea salt

01 Pre-heat oven to 425°F.

02 In a large bowl, add flour, sugar, flax seeds, sea salt, black pepper, garlic powder, basil, and baking powder. Whisk with a pastry cutter or whisk to incorporate all the ingredients. Cut ¼ cup vegan butter into mixture with pastry cutter, until mixture appears crumbly. Add in almond or soymilk. Mix until just incorporated. The dough will not be completely smooth.

03 Roll dough on floured surface into ½ inch thick square. Cut into 4-6 circles (2-3 inches in diameter) with biscuit cutter. Place on parchment lined baking sheet. Brush tops of biscuits with maple syrup. Bake for about 18 minutes, or until golden brown.

04 In a mixing bowl, whisk VeganEgg powder with ice-cold water, sea salt and pepper until smooth and slightly thickened.

*(Ingredients & Directions continued on next page)*

*(Continued from previous page)*

¼ teaspoon ground black pepper

2 teaspoons, plus 2 teaspoons vegan butter

4-6 vegan breakfast sausage patties

4-6 slices Follow Your Heart American Slices

05 Heat a non-stick skillet over medium heat add 2 teaspoons vegan butter. Gently pour VeganEgg mixture into pan and spread out evenly and do not agitate. Cook 4 minutes, then flip and cook 3-4 more minutes.

06 Meanwhile, heat a sauté pan over medium heat and add additional 2 teaspoons vegan butter. Add sausages and cook until warm. Set aside.

07 When biscuits are still slightly warm, cut open and add slice of Follow Your Heart American cheese, 1 sausage patty and a folded portion of VeganEgg. Repeat for all biscuits. Serve warm.

# Breakfast Tacos with Creamy Tomatillo Sauce

## BY RASHI BHATNAGAR

**YIELDS:** 8 Tacos   **DIFFICULTY:** Easy to Moderate
**PREP TIME:** 10 Minutes   **COOK TIME:** 15 Minutes

## TOOLS YOU'LL NEED

**Tacos are life! The many sauces in this recipe harmoniously come together in a tangy, spicy fusion that satisfies every taste bud. The addition of hearty black beans and VeganEgg ensure that these tacos will keep you satisfied until lunchtime. (Gluten-Free)**

### Creamy Tomatillo Sauce Ingredients

1 cup pre-made tomatillo salsa

1 ½ tablespoons fresh lemon juice

1 avocado, diced

½ cup fresh cilantro, roughly chopped, plus more for garnish *Optional

½ teaspoon sea salt

### Taco Ingredients

½ cup VeganEgg powder

2 cup ice-cold water

¼ teaspoon sea salt

¼ teaspoon ground black pepper

1 tablespoon neutral-tasting oil (safflower)

½ cup canned black beans, rinsed and drained

2 teaspoons fresh lemon juice

01   To a blender, add tomatillo salsa, lemon juice, avocado, ½ cup cilantro, and sea salt. Blend until smooth. Set aside.

02   In a mixing bowl, add VeganEgg powder, ice-cold water, sea salt and pepper and whisk until smooth and slightly thickened, about 1 minute. Set aside.

03   Follow cooking directions for The Perfect Scramble (Page 10).

04   Add black beans to scramble and cook about 2 minutes, or until heated through. Turn off heat and add lemon juice.

05   Heat tortillas on a dry pan until pliable and warm. Spread desired amount of Chipotle Vegenaise on each tortilla.

06   For each tortilla, add a few tablespoons scrambled VeganEgg, desired amount red onions and cabbage. Drizzle each taco with Creamy Tomatillo sauce and red salsa.

*(Ingredients & Directions continued on next page)*

*(Continued from previous page)*

Assembly

8 corn tortillas

2 tablespoons Chipotle Vegenaise

2 tablespoons red onion, finely chopped

1 cup shredded red cabbage

¼ cup pre-made red salsa

2 tablespoons hot sauce *Optional

07 Garnish with additional cilantro, if desired. Serve with hot sauce on side, if using.

# MAIN *Meals*

## LUNCH *and* DINNER

"Ham," VeganEgg, & Cheese Puffs ........................................ 50

Mashed Potato Waffles ............................................................ 52

Spanish Omelette (Tortilla Española) .................................. 56

Fresh Homemade Pasta ......................................................... 60

Summertime Tomato & Basil Pasta ..................................... 64

Scrambled VeganEgg Salad .................................................. 66

Classic Fried Rice with Scrambled VeganEgg ................. 68

Lentil Meatballs ......................................................................... 70

Smoky Eggplant Burgers ....................................................... 74

Vegan Matzo Ball Soup ......................................................... 78

# "Ham," VeganEgg, & Cheese Puffs

## BY SPORK FOODS

**YIELDS:** 6 Large Puffs  **DIFFICULTY:** Easy
**PREP TIME:** 10-15 Minutes  **COOK TIME:** 30 Minutes

### TOOLS YOU'LL NEED

**This simple and savory pastry appetizer is sure to be a crowd-pleaser! Slice them into strips for your next party and we guarantee that your serving dish will come home clean.**

1 package vegan puff pastry, thawed

6 slices Follow Your Heart American Slices

12 vegan ham deli slices

4 tablespoons VeganEgg powder

½ cup ice-cold water

½ cup soymilk creamer

½ teaspoon sea salt

¼ teaspoon ground black pepper

2 teaspoons lemon juice

2 tablespoons, plus 2 tablespoons
fresh chives, finely chopped

01  Thaw puff pastry according to directions.

02  Preheat oven to 400°F.

03  Slice each sheet puff pastry into three long strips, about 3 x 8 inches. Bake empty on parchment lined baking sheet for 8-10 minutes.

04  Meanwhile, slice ham into strips and dice Follow Your Heart American Slices. Set aside.

05  In a mixing bowl, whisk VeganEgg with ice-cold water, creamer, sea salt, pepper and lemon juice. Whisk until smooth and slightly thickened, about 1 minute. Fold in 2 tablespoons chives.

06  Gently crack center of baked puff pastry strips lengthwise and spoon in 3 tablespoons VeganEgg mixture per strip. Top each strip with diced Follow Your Heart American Slices (equivalent of 1 slice) and then ham strips (equivalent of 2 slices).

07  Bake for 18-20 minutes, or until edges are golden. Serve warm and top with additional chives.

# Mashed Potato Waffles

## BY CAROLYN SCOTT-HAMILTON @healthyvoyager

**SERVES:** 4-6 **DIFFICULTY:** Moderate
**PREP TIME:** 20 Minutes **COOK TIME:** 10-20 Minutes

### TOOLS YOU'LL NEED

You might not think to put mashed potatoes into a waffle iron, but this recipe deliciously defies that logic. The melted Cheddar cheese, chives, and garlic all combine with the potatoes to form a wonderfully crispy and savory waffle, perfect for smothering with our vegan sour cream. It's addicting!

2-3 russet potatoes, peeled and diced (2 ½ cups mashed potatoes used)

¼ cup almond, soy or cashew milk

¼ teaspoon lemon juice

¼ cup VeganEgg powder

1 cup ice-cold water

2 tablespoons vegetable oil

3 tablespoons scallions or chives, finely chopped, plus 2 tablespoons for topping

½ cup Follow Your Heart Cheddar Cheese shreds

1 teaspoon garlic powder

½ teaspoon sea salt

¼ teaspoon ground black pepper

1 ¼ – 1 ½ cups all-purpose flour

½ teaspoon baking powder

¼ teaspoon baking soda

⅓ cup Follow Your Heart Sour Cream

01 Bring 6 cups salted water to a boil. Add diced potatoes. Cook about 15 minutes until easily poked with fork. Drain and mash. Set aside 2 ½ cups mashed potatoes to cool.

02 Meanwhile, place almond, soy or cashew milk in bowl and whisk with lemon juice. Whisk and set aside to curdle, 1-2 minutes, creating vegan buttermilk.

03 Pre-heat waffle iron and grease with cooking spray.

04 In a mixing bowl, add VeganEgg powder and ice-cold water. Whisk until smooth and slightly thickened, about 1 minute. Set aside.

05 In large bowl, whisk together oil, vegan buttermilk and VeganEgg mixture. Stir in mashed potatoes, scallions and cheese until well combined. Add garlic powder, sea salt and pepper.

06 In a separate small bowl, whisk together flour, baking powder and baking soda. Fold flour mixture into potato mixture until well combined.

*(Directions continued on next page)*

*(Continued from previous page)*

07 Scoop mixture onto prepared waffle iron, spreading it into an even layer in center of iron. Potato mixture will not spread or expand as much as a traditional waffle, so spread closer to edge than traditional batter. Bake until golden brown. If waffle is too wet, add more flour to the mixture, 1 tablespoon at a time until desired consistency is reached. Repeat for all remaining potato batter. Serve waffles warm with sour cream and scallions or chives.

# Spanish Omelette (Tortilla Española)

## BY ERIN WYSOCARSKI @olivesfordinner

**SERVES:** 4  **DIFFICULTY:** Moderate
**PREP TIME:** 10 Minutes  **COOK TIME:** 22 Minutes

### TOOLS YOU'LL NEED

"A traditional Spanish omelette has three components: eggs, potatoes and onion. The VeganEgg here provides a fluffy, eggy base that nestles perfectly between lightly caramelized onions and paper-thin potato slices. This simple but delicious dish tastes amazing straight out of the pan piping hot or lightly reheated the next day as leftovers." – OLIVES FOR DINNER (Gluten-Free)

1 medium white onion, thinly sliced

1 medium waxy potato (Yukon gold), thinly sliced

3 tablespoons olive oil, divided

½ cup VeganEgg powder

2 cups ice-cold water,

½ teaspoon sea salt

¼ teaspoon finely ground black pepper

¼ cup fresh parsley, finely chopped, divided

01  To thinly slice onion and potato, use a mandoline slicer or use the slicing blade of a food processor, on a thin setting. Set aside.

02  Heat 1 tablespoon olive oil in a large skillet over medium heat. Add sliced onions and allow to soften for about 5 minutes, or until slightly browned. Remove from heat (reserving pan) and transfer to a bowl. Set aside.

03  Heat another tablespoon olive oil to same pan and add sliced potatoes. Allow to cook for several minutes, or until soft and slightly golden around edges. Remove from pan, and add to bowl with onions.

04  Heat remaining tablespoon of oil in a small (6-inch) cast iron pan over medium heat.

05  While the oil is heating, whisk VeganEgg powder and ice-cold water together in a large bowl, until smooth and slightly thickened, about 1 minute. Season with sea salt and black pepper, then add onions, potatoes and two tablespoons fresh parsley to bowl and stir gently to combine.

*(Directions continued on next page)*

*(Continued from previous page)*

06   Pour entire mixture into cast-iron pan and allow to cook for 6-8 minutes.

07   To flip, dab gently with paper towel to remove excess oil. Place a plate with a larger circumference than pan over top, and turn upside-down*. Then, place edge of plate into edge of pan farthest from you and slide it back into the pan, allowing it to cook for an additional 6-8 minutes. *Don't worry if the contents spill out a bit when you flip it. Simply reshape it gently with a spatula once you return it to the pan – it will firm up more as it cooks.

08   It's done when it's flipped onto a plate again and holds its shape. If it's still a bit loose after cooking it on both sides, reduce the heat a bit and allow it to cook for a few to several more minutes on each side.

09   Allow omelette to rest and cool for a few minutes before slicing. Garnish with remaining parsley, and extra salt and pepper, if desired.

# Fresh Homemade Pasta

## BY CHEF TAL RONNEN @crossroadskitchen

**SERVES:** 4-6   **DIFFICULTY:** Advanced
**PREP TIME:** 40 Minutes + Chilling Time   **COOK TIME:** 10 Minutes

### TOOLS YOU'LL NEED

Fun fact: "00" flour is also called doppio zero flour, referring to how finely the flour is ground. "00" flour is recommended for homemade pasta (and pizza dough), though, if you are in a pinch, all-purpose flour will technically work. Note: Fettucine and spaghetti should be rolled out thicker than stuffed pastas like ravioli. Skip the store-bought pasta sauce and instead toss with fresh ingredients to highlight the amazing work you just put into to making your very own homemade pasta. (Try our next recipe for Summertime Tomato & Basil Pasta)

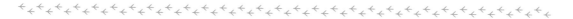

¼ cup VeganEgg powder

1 cup ice-cold water

1 ½ cups "00" flour, plus more for rolling dough

1 ½ cups unbleached all-purpose flour

½ teaspoon sea salt

¼ cup water

01   Add VeganEgg powder to a mixing bowl and add 1 cup ice-cold water. Whisk until smooth and slightly thickened, about 1 minute. Set aside.

02   To a food processor, add flours and salt. Pulse to incorporate a few times. Slowly add in VeganEgg mixture and additional water. Continue to pulse until dough ball forms. Dough should feel moist but not sticky.

03   Remove half of dough ball and cover with plastic wrap. Pulse remaining half of dough ball in food processor until smooth and elastic. Remove from food processor and work remaining half of dough.

04   Wrap dough in plastic wrap and let sit 30-60 minutes.

05   Sprinkle clean surface with "00" flour. Divide dough into 2 pieces and set aside remaining half by wrapping back in plastic.

06   Roll slightly into long oblong shape with rolling pin, until about ½ inch thick.

*(Directions continued on next page)*

*(Continued from previous page)*

07    Using the flat roller on pasta maker, feed through largest opening setting, using your hand to support the dough as it feeds through.

08    Fold ends of dough toward the middle so they overlap (also called laminating) and stretch with rolling pin to a narrow sheet that will again fit through pasta maker.

09    Using second largest setting on pasta maker, feed through until pasta is desired thickness.

10    Place fettuccini or spaghetti cutting attachment onto pasta maker, if using, and gently feed dough through, ensuring there is enough flour to prevent dough from sticking. You can also cut your pasta into strips by hand.

11    Once long noodles are created, lay on floured board or baking sheet to dry out. Alternately, hang to dry, about ½ hour. Repeat for remaining piece of dough.

12    To cook, bring salted water to a boil. For most varieties of pasta, boil for about 2 minutes, or until noodles float to surface.

# Summertime Tomato & Basil Pasta

## BY SPORK FOODS

**SERVES:** 4-6  **DIFFICULTY:** Easy
**PREP TIME:** 5 Minutes  **COOK TIME:** 10 Minutes

### TOOLS YOU'LL NEED

When you make your own pasta, you want to serve it in a way that showcases its superb fresh taste and texture. This sauce is so simple and classic that your efforts on that homemade pasta will be exquisitely highlighted and you'll have twice the bragging rights!

2 tablespoons olive oil

3 large cloves garlic, finely chopped

1 cup cherry tomatoes, quartered

12-14 leaves fresh basil, thinly sliced

juice of 1 lemon

2 lemons, zested

Fresh Homemade Pasta (Page 60)

01  In a sauté pan, add oil and heat over medium-low. Add garlic and cook about 30 seconds.

02  Add tomatoes and cook 1 more minute.

03  Remove from heat and toss with pasta.

04  Add basil, lemon juice and zest and toss to coat. Serve warm.

# Scrambled VeganEgg Salad

## BY JACKIE POLES RAN @beinvegan

**SERVES:** 4-6  **DIFFICULTY:** Easy
**PREP TIME:** 10 Minutes   **COOK TIME:** 8 Minutes

## TOOLS YOU'LL NEED

Egg salad is a refreshing summertime go-to treat and we've cooked up a vegan version made with scrambled VeganEgg that will knock you off your picnic bench. Relax in the sunshine and enjoy the traditional tangy mustard, fresh dill, and creamy Vegenaise as you devour every last bite. (Gluten-Free)

¾ cup VeganEgg powder

2 ½ cups ice-cold water

¼ teaspoon sea salt

¼ teaspoon ground black pepper

2 teaspoons neutral-tasting oil for pan (safflower)

½ cup Follow Your Heart Vegenaise

1 tablespoon Dijon mustard

½ tablespoon lemon juice

⅛ teaspoon paprika

½ teaspoon white wine vinegar

¼ cup red onion, small dice

¼ cup celery, small dice

1 tablespoon capers

1 tablespoon fresh dill, finely chopped

01  To a mixing bowl, add VeganEgg powder, ice-cold water, sea salt, and pepper. Whisk until smooth and slightly thickened, about 1 minute.

02  Follow cooking directions for The Perfect Scramble (Page 10).

03  Set cooked VeganEggs aside in a mixing bowl while preparing sauce.

04  In a separate bowl, add Vegenaise, mustard, lemon juice, paprika, white wine vinegar and whisk gently, just until uniform. Pour over scrambled VeganEggs and fold in gently to incorporate.

05  Fold in red onion, celery, capers, and dill.

06  Season to taste with additional salt and pepper, if desired. Refrigerate to chill or eat immediately on top of a toasted bagel, English muffin, or with bread as a sandwich.

# Classic Fried Rice with Scrambled VeganEgg

## BY SPORK FOODS

**SERVES:** 4-6   **DIFFICULTY:** Moderate
**PREP TIME:** 15 Minutes   **COOK TIME:** 22 Minutes + Rice Cooking Time

### TOOLS YOU'LL NEED

**Who needs Chinese take-out when you've got this recipe for fried rice made with scrambled VeganEgg? The classic flavors of tamari, rice vinegar, and toasted sesame oil combined with freshly chopped onion, carrots, and peas will make this fried rice your new favorite weeknight meal. (Gluten-Free)**

---

1 ½ cups short grain brown rice

2 tablespoons neutral-tasting oil (safflower)

½ white onion, finely chopped

½ red bell pepper, small dice

2 medium orange carrots, small dice

½ cup fresh or frozen green peas (thawed)

1 tablespoon, plus 2 teaspoons wheat-free tamari

1 tablespoon rice vinegar

2 teaspoons, plus 1 teaspoon toasted sesame oil

¼ cup VeganEgg powder

1 cup ice-cold water

¼ teaspoon ground black pepper

2 tablespoons green onion, finely chopped *Optional

**01**  Cook brown rice according to package. Set aside. This can be made a day ahead and refrigerated.

**02**  Heat a large sauté pan over medium high, and add 2 tablespoons oil. Add onion and sauté for about 1 minute. Add bell pepper, carrots and peas and cook for about 2-4 minutes, stirring once. Add rice and sauté, coating rice well in the oil. Add 1 tablespoon tamari, rice vinegar and 2 teaspoons sesame oil. Stir to evenly coat and cook about 5-7 minutes at medium heat, stirring occasionally, until heated through. Remove from heat.

**03**  Add VeganEgg powder to a mixing bowl and whisk in ice-cold water. Whisk until smooth and slightly thickened, about 1 minute. Whisk in 2 teaspoons tamari, 1 teaspoon sesame oil and black pepper.

**04**  Follow cooking directions for The Perfect Scramble (Page 10).

**05**  Cool slightly and fold into rice mixture. Garnish with chopped green onion, if using. Serve warm.

# Lentil Meatballs

## BY COLLEEN PATRICK-GOUDREAU @joyfulvegan

**YIELDS:** Approx. 20 Meatballs   **DIFFICULTY:** Moderate
**PREP TIME:** 15-20 Minutes + Chilling Time   **COOK TIME:** 20-30 Minutes

### TOOLS YOU'LL NEED

*"Of course there are commercial vegan meatballs in the store, but this recipe allows you to enjoy a much more delicious and healthy meatball. Whichever you choose, they're heads above animal-based versions when we use compassion and health as our barometers!"* – **COLLEEN**  You'll want to start this recipe with your lentils already cooked. Brown lentils take about 25 minutes to cook (no pre-soaking required).

2 tablespoons olive oil, divided

1 yellow onion, finely chopped

2-3 garlic cloves, minced

2 ½ cups cooked brown lentils

2 level tablespoons VeganEgg powder

½ cup ice-cold water

¼ cup non-dairy unsweetened milk

½ cup breadcrumbs (Italian-style or plain)

¼ cup fresh parsley, finely chopped

¼ cup Follow Your Heart Parmesan cheese or nutritional yeast

1 tablespoon dried oregano

1 teaspoon sea salt, plus pinch

½ teaspoon ground black pepper

marinara sauce of your choice

**01** Heat up one tablespoon of oil in a large sauté pan, and add onion. Sauté over medium-high heat until onion is translucent, about 5-7 minutes. Sprinkle with a pinch of sea salt, add garlic, and sauté for another minute. Turn off heat and set aside.

**02** Add cooked lentils to a large bowl. Use a fork or potato masher to mash lentils. Alternately, if using a food processor, only use the pulse setting to acquire soft and mashed lentils, not a paste.

**03** In a small bowl, whisk VeganEgg powder and ice-cold water until smooth and slightly thickened, about 1 minute. Set aside.

**04** To mashed lentils, add prepared VeganEgg mixture, milk, and breadcrumbs. Add onion/garlic mixture, parsley, Parmesan or nutritional yeast, oregano, sea salt, and pepper. Mix with a wooden spoon to combine. Let mixture rest in the refrigerator for a few hours to overnight, not to exceed 12 hours.

*(Directions continued on next page)*

*(Continued from previous page)*

05　When ready to prepare, squish mixture with hands. The mixture should be quite wet and able to be formed into balls that will stay together when cooked. If it's too wet, add some more breadcrumbs. If it's too dry, add a little more milk. Taste and add more salt or other seasoning, if desired.

06　Shape lentil mixture into balls of your desired size. You can make them large like a golf ball or smaller. You can also use a melon baller or small ice cream scoop to create uniform sizes.

07　Next, add remaining tablespoon of olive oil to the same large sauté pan you used to sauté the onions, and turn your stove to medium heat. Brown lentil balls on all sides. If using right away, add them to a large pot of marinara sauce. If not using right away, store them in an airtight container for up to three days.

08　Serve with pasta and your favorite marinara sauce or on a hearty roll with sauce and vegan cheese for a meatball sub!

**FYI:** A good rule of thumb when cooking brown lentils on a stovetop is to use 2 ½ cups of liquid (water, stock, etc.) to 1 cup of dry lentils. Bring to a boil, cover tightly, reduce heat and simmer until they are tender, about 20 to 25 minutes. Season with salt, and serve. This will yield the 2 ½ cups of lentils you need for this recipe.

# Smoky Eggplant Burgers

## BY BRIAN PATTON @thesexyvegan

**YIELDS:** Serves 4   **DIFFICULTY:** Moderate to Advanced
**PREP TIME:** 15-20 Minutes   **COOK TIME:** 60 Minutes

## TOOLS YOU'LL NEED

*"Roasting eggplant over an open flame imparts a natural smokiness and tenderizes it perfectly. The meaty texture of eggplant makes it the perfect choice for a vegan burger and the binding power of the VeganEgg helps hold all of this deliciousness together. If you don't have gas burners, you can roast the eggplant under the broiler or on a BBQ grill." – BRIAN  (Gluten-Free with gluten-free panko crumbs and hamburger buns)*

### Burger Ingredients

1 cup cooked short grain brown rice

1 medium eggplant

¾ cup panko bread crumbs

½ cup walnuts coarsely ground

2 tablespoons chopped Italian parsley

2 teaspoons granulated garlic

2 teaspoons granulated onion

1 tablespoon smoked paprika

2 teaspoons dried oregano

1 teaspoon sea salt

¼ teaspoon pepper

2 level tablespoons VeganEgg powder

½ cup ice-cold water

1 tablespoon refined coconut oil

### Lemon-Pepper Dijonnaise

¼ cup Vegenaise

2 teaspoons Dijon mustard

**01** If using a gas stove, turn burner to high, and place eggplant directly on flame. Roast 10 to 12 minutes turning frequently with tongs, until skin is blackened and starting to flake off all around, and eggplant is very tender.

If using an oven, slice eggplant in half lengthwise and place on a baking sheet with the skin facing up. Roast under the broiler for about 15-20 minutes until the skins are charred and eggplant is tender.

**02** Place eggplant in a bowl, and cover with plastic. Let it sit, covered, for at least 20 minutes, then peel off, and discard skin. There will be little black flecks of skin all around, this is desirable. Discard any liquid that has collected in bottom of bowl. Cut off stem and roughly chop eggplant (you should have about 1 cup) and place in a medium mixing bowl.

**03** Add rice, breadcrumbs, walnuts, parsley, garlic, onion, paprika, oregano, sea salt and pepper to bowl with eggplant. Smoosh it all together with

*(Ingredients & Directions continued on next page)*

Zest of 1 lemon

2 teaspoons minced chives

¼ teaspoon coarsely ground pepper

*Assez*

4 hamburger buns

Lemon-Pepper Dijonnaise (recipe in step 05)

1 cup shredded romaine lettuce

4 slices beefsteak tomato (¼ inch thick)

¼ cup red onion, thinly sliced

your hand until it is combined. Taste mixture and add salt and pepper to taste.

04  To a small mixing bowl, add VeganEgg powder, and ice-cold water. Whisk until smooth and slightly thickened, about 1 minute. Fold in VeganEgg mixture into eggplant mixture until well combined. Cover and refrigerate for 30 minutes.

05  For the Lemon-Pepper Dijonnaise, in a small mixing bowl, add Vegenaise, mustard, lemon zest, chives, and pepper. Whisk to combine. Season with salt and pepper to taste.

06  Pre-heat oven to 425°F.

07  In a large, oven-safe skillet (preferably cast iron or non-stick) heat oil to medium. Divide burger mixture into 4 equal portions and form into thick round patties. Place patties in pan. They should sizzle. Cook on one side for 3 to 4 minutes until browned. Flip burgers, then immediately place pan in oven on the middle rack, and bake for 30 minutes. Remove and let rest for 2 minutes.

08  To build burgers: smear top and bottom of the bun with Lemon-Pepper Dijonnaise. Add the burger patty, then top with lettuce, tomato, and onion.

# Vegan Matzo Ball Soup

## BY JACKIE POLES RAN @beinvegan

**YIELDS:** 16-18 Matzo Balls  **SERVES:** 6-8  **DIFFICULTY:** Moderate
**PREP TIME:** 10 Minutes + Chilling Time  **COOK TIME:** 45 Minutes

## TOOLS YOU'LL NEED

Come Passover, matzo ball soup is by far the family favorite. The trick with these is to let your matzo balls cook in the pot without disturbing them: don't peek under the lid, don't stir them, just leave them be.

### Matzo Ball Ingredients

1 ½ cups matzo meal

1 teaspoon kosher salt

2 teaspoons baking powder

1 teaspoon onion powder

1 teaspoon garlic powder

1 teaspoon dried parsley

1 teaspoon dried dill

¼ teaspoon ground black pepper, plus to taste

½ cup VeganEgg powder

1 ½ cups ice-cold water

2 tablespoons safflower oil

### Soup Ingredients

1 tablespoon vegan butter

1 onion, diced

2 cloves garlic, finely chopped

3 carrots, cut into thin rounds

2 stalks celery, diced

8 cups vegan "no chicken" style broth

01  To a mixing bowl, add matzo meal, kosher salt, baking powder, onion powder, garlic powder, parsley, dill, and black pepper. Whisk.

02  In a separate mixing bowl, add VeganEgg powder and ice-cold water. Whisk until smooth and slightly thickened, about 1 minute. Add oil to VeganEgg mixture and gently mix to combine.

03  Pour VeganEgg mixture into dry mixture and gently combine until uniform. Do not over mix.

04  Cover and place in refrigerator for about 1 hour to firm up.

05  Bring a large pot of salted water to a boil.

06  After matzo ball mixture has set, scoop about 2 tablespoons matzo ball mixture and roll into balls. Add to boiling water and cover.

07  Continue to boil until all balls float to top, then lower water to a simmer and cook for 40 minutes. Keep the lid on, and do not stir at any time. Leave the matzo balls be!

08  Meanwhile, place vegan butter in separate stock pot and heat over medium heat. Add onion,

*(Ingredients and Directions continued on next page)*

*(Continued from previous page)*

⅓ cup fresh dill, roughly chopped

½ teaspoon sea salt, plus to taste

¼ teaspoon finely ground black pepper, plus to taste

garlic, carrots and celery and cook until translucent, about 5 minutes. Reduce heat to medium-low and add broth, fresh dill, sea salt and pepper. Cook until warmed through.

09 Remove matzo balls from water with a slotted spoon and serve warm in soup! Season to taste with sea salt and pepper.

# TASTY

## *Treats*

### DESSERTS *and* SWEETS

Rich Chocolate Brownies .................................................. 84

Soft-Batch Chocolate Chip Cookies .................................. 88

Prosecco-Battered Apple Fritters .................................... 90

Challah ........................................................................... 92

Orange Cranberry Baked Donuts .................................... 96

Chocolate Bread Pudding .............................................. 100

Chocolate Cupcakes with Cream Cheese Filling ........ 104

Spiced Banana Bread with Toasted Hazelnuts............ 108

Vanilla Bean Custard ..................................................... 110

# Rich Chocolate Brownies

## BY SPORK FOODS

**YIELDS:** 12 Brownies   **DIFFICULTY:** Moderate
**PREP TIME:** 10-15 Minutes   **COOK TIME:** 30 Minutes

### TOOLS YOU'LL NEED

We like chocolate. A lot. And who doesn't want to be rich when it comes to chocolate! Made with velvety dark chocolate, these lush little squares will make you feel like a millionaire.

¾ cup dark chocolate chips, plus ¼ cup for topping

2 tablespoons VeganEgg powder

1 ¼ cup unsweetened ice-cold almond milk

½ cup vegan butter, softened

½ cup evaporated cane sugar

1 teaspoon vanilla extract

1 ½ cup unbleached all-purpose flour

½ cup unsweetened cocoa powder

½ teaspoon baking powder

½ teaspoon sea salt

¼ teaspoon ground cinnamon

**01**   Pre-heat oven to 350°F. Grease an 8-inch square pan.

**02**   Melt chocolate chips in a double boiler, or heat-proof bowl over a small pot, with 1 inch of simmering water. Smooth with spatula until chips are melted and creamy.

**03**   In a mixing bowl, whisk VeganEgg powder and ice-cold almond milk until smooth and slightly thickened, about 1 minute.

**04**   In a large mixing bowl with a pastry whisk, or stand mixer fitted with a paddle attachment cream together vegan butter, sugar, vanilla extract and VeganEgg mixture.

**05**   In a separate bowl, whisk flour, cocoa powder, baking powder, sea salt and cinnamon. Once mixture is uniform, add dry ingredients and melted chocolate to creamed ingredients. Whisk gently until uniform. The mixture should be like a thick cake batter.

**06**   Add batter to pan and spread out evenly. Sprinkle on ¼ cup chocolate chips to top of batter. Gently press down chips into batter.

*(Directions continued on next page)*

*(Continued from previous page)*

**07** Bake for about 30 minutes, until top looks slightly dry and a toothpick comes out clean when inserted in the center (taking care not to insert your toothpick into a melted chocolate chip).

# Soft-Batch Chocolate Chip Cookies

## BY SPORK FOODS

**YIELDS:** 12 Cookies   **DIFFICULTY:** Easy
**PREP TIME:** 10 Minutes   **COOK TIME:** 25-27 Minutes

### TOOLS YOU'LL NEED

We know. Chocolate chip cookies are nothing new to the vegan dessert tray and there are definitely some killer ones out there. But when you mix in a VeganEgg, a little extra almond milk, and some Spork Foods magic, you get these scrumptiously light and fluffy soft-batch cookies that may soon become your favorite.

2 tablespoons VeganEgg powder

¼ cup ice-cold water

½ cup vegan butter, softened

¾ cup evaporated cane sugar

2 teaspoons vanilla extract

¼ teaspoon sea salt

¼ teaspoon ground cinnamon

⅛ teaspoon ground allspice

1 ½ cups unbleached all-purpose flour

3 tablespoons unsweetened almond milk

½ cup dark chocolate chips

**01** Preheat oven to 350°F.

**02** In a small bowl, add VeganEgg powder and ice-cold water. Whisk until smooth and slightly thickened, about 1 minute. Set aside.

**03** In a large bowl, or stand mixer fitted with paddle attachment, cream together vegan butter and sugar, until well mixed. Add VeganEgg mixture, vanilla extract, sea salt, cinnamon, and allspice. Mix until uniform.

**04** Add flour and almond milk. Mix until all ingredients look evenly distributed. Fold in chocolate chips.

**05** Using a heaping tablespoon measure, scoop batter onto greased baking sheet, or silicone lined sheet. Space about 2 inches apart and press gently to flatten slightly.

**06** Bake for about 25-27 minutes. Cool completely on a wire rack. To preserve their texture, store cookies in a metal tin in the refrigerator for the best consistency.

# Prosecco-Battered Apple Fritters

## BY OLIVIA ROSZKOWSKI FOR NATURALLY, DANNY SEO

**YIELDS:** 24-26 Fritters   **DIFFICULTY:** Moderate
**PREP TIME:** 10 Minutes   **COOK TIME:** 8-10 Minutes

### TOOLS YOU'LL NEED

As though they've fallen from a tree of decadence, we can't deny that these apple fritters are worth an extra 20 minutes on the treadmill. Just be sure to savor every bite and take an extra sip of that leftover prosecco!

### Dry Ingredients

¼ cup VeganEgg powder

¾ cup unbleached all-purpose flour

¼ cup coconut sugar (or sugar of choice)

½ teaspoon ground cinnamon

1 teaspoon baking powder

⅛ teaspoon sea salt

### To Form Batter

2 apples, cored and diced small (3 cups)

½ teaspoon vanilla extract

¾ cup prosecco

### For Frying

1-2 cups refined coconut oil (or safflower), to fry

### For Dusting

¼ cup organic powdered sugar

**01** Whisk the VeganEgg powder, flour, coconut sugar, cinnamon, baking powder, and sea salt in a medium bowl to combine.

**02** Toss diced apples into mixture, making sure each piece is coated.

**03** Heat 1-inch of oil in a medium pot, until temperature reaches 350°F.

**04** Pour in the vanilla extract and prosecco into apple mixture and fold gently until combined.

**05** Working in batches, carefully place heaping tablespoons of batter into the oil and cook for 2-4 minutes, or until golden, turning once. Use a slotted spoon to remove fritters from oil.

**06** Place on rack to cool slightly and dust with powdered sugar before serving.

# Challah

## BY FOLLOW YOUR HEART

**YIELDS:** 1 Loaf   **DIFFICULTY:** Easy
**PREP TIME:** 30 Minutes + 2 Hours Proofing   **COOK TIME:** 35-45 Minutes

## TOOLS YOU'LL NEED

Challah is a soft, slightly sweet bread whose characteristic braiding makes it a beautiful addition to your dinner table. Traditionally made with eggs, similar to a Brioche, this bread maintains its pillowy texture thanks to VeganEgg and gets its distinctive shine from the maple syrup brushed on top.

1 ½ – 1 ¾ cups lukewarm unsweetened almond milk

¾ cup evaporated cane sugar

1 packet (2 ½ teaspoons) Active Dry Yeast

2 tablespoons VeganEgg powder

½ cup ice-cold unsweetened almond milk

6 – 6 ¼ cups unbleached all-purpose flour

¼ teaspoon turmeric

1 teaspoon sea salt

½ cup neutral-tasting oil (safflower), plus additional oil for coating bowl

2 tablespoons maple syrup

2 tablespoons unsweetened almond milk

Poppy seeds and/or sesame seeds, for sprinkling on top

**01**  Mix together 1 ½ cups lukewarm almond milk, sugar, and yeast in a small bowl. Set aside for 7-10 minutes so yeast can blossom and become bubbly.

**02**  In a small bowl, add VeganEgg powder and ice-cold almond milk. Whisk until smooth and slightly thickened, about 1 minute. Set aside.

**03**  In a large stand mixer, mix flour, turmeric, and sea salt to combine. Using a dough hook at low speed, add oil, VeganEgg mixture, and blossomed yeast mixture to the flour blend. Mix until smooth dough forms (about 1-2 minutes). You want the dough to feel soft but not sticky. You may find that you need to add a little extra flour or milk to achieve the right texture. Then remove dough from bowl and knead on a floured surface for an additional 2 minutes.

**04**  If using oven to proof the dough, preheat to 100°F and then turn off oven just before you insert dough for proofing. If not using oven, place dough in a warm place. Place rounded dough into a large oiled bowl. Cover with damp towel and let double in size for about 1 hour.

*(Directions continued on next page)*

*(Continued from previous page)*

**05** Place dough on a floured surface and cut into three equal pieces. With your hands, roll each piece into long strands (about 18 inches) and let set for 5 minutes, then transfer to baking sheet. Bunch ends together and braid Challah.

**06** In a small bowl, whisk maple syrup with remaining 2 tablespoons almond milk. Brush your braided Challah loaf evenly with half of the maple syrup glaze. Set aside to rise for about 35-45 minutes, until dough slowly pushes back when you gently poke with your finger. Meanwhile, preheat oven to 375°F.

**07** Brush loaf with maple syrup mixture one more time, sprinkle with poppy and/or sesame seeds, and bake for 40 minutes until top is golden brown and a firm crust has formed. Let cool on baking sheet for 10 minutes before transferring to a wire cooling rack and cool completely before slicing.

# Orange Cranberry Baked Donuts

## BY GABRIELLE ST. CLAIRE @eat.drink.shrink

**YIELDS:** 12 Donuts  **DIFFICULTY:** Moderate
**PREP TIME:** 15 Minutes  **COOK TIME:** 20-30 Minutes

## TOOLS YOU'LL NEED

Donuts?! Did someone say donuts? A donut baking pan is a fun new addition to your kitchen, especially when you have this elegant and mouthwatering recipe. Just be sure to share because no one can eat 12 donuts. We tried. Note: These donuts can be stored in an airtight container for up to 3 days – but they're best served fresh.

2 tablespoons VeganEgg powder

½ cup ice-cold water

½ cup unsweetened non-dairy milk

1 teaspoon apple cider vinegar

1 teaspoon almond extract

1 ½ cups unbleached all-purpose flour, sifted

½ teaspoon sea salt

½ cup coconut sugar

1 ½ teaspoon baking powder

1 tablespoon orange juice

Zest of 1 orange (about 2 ½ teaspoons)

⅓ cup coconut oil, softened

½ cup dried cranberries

### Orange Glaze

1 cup powdered sugar

2 tablespoons orange juice

Zest of ½ orange (1 ½ teaspoons)

01  Preheat oven to 350°F and grease donut pan, and set aside.

02  In a mixing bowl, add VeganEgg powder and ice-cold water. Whisk until smooth and slightly thickened, about 1 minute. Set aside.

03  Combine non-dairy milk with apple cider vinegar and whisk. Set aside a few minutes to curdle. Then add almond extract and set aside.

04  In a separate bowl, whisk flour, sea salt, sugar, and baking powder.

05  In a large bowl or stand mixer, add dry ingredients, then add curdled non-dairy milk, orange juice and zest, coconut oil, and VeganEgg mixture. Continue to mix. Beat for 30 seconds and scrape down side of bowl as needed. Once combined, add in dried cranberries and distribute evenly.

06  Transfer batter into greased pan, carefully filling each donut indentation about ¾ full. Bake 20-30 minutes, or until toothpick comes out clean and donuts are golden brown.

*(Directions continued on next page)*

*(Continued from previous page)*

**07** Remove from pan and allow to cool in pan on a wire rack, for about 7-10 minutes. Invert donuts onto wire rack and let cool completely before glazing.

**08** For the glaze, in a small bowl, whisk together powdered sugar and orange juice until smooth.

**09** Place wax paper under wire rack to collect drippings for easy cleanup. Dip top of each donut into icing and transfer to wire rack and lightly top with orange zest. Let set for 5 minutes. Serve immediately.

# Chocolate Bread Pudding

## BY JACKIE POLES RAN @beinvegan

**SERVES:** 6-8  **DIFFICULTY:** Easy
**PREP TIME:** 12 Minutes  **COOK TIME:** 60 Minutes

### TOOLS YOU'LL NEED

Bread, good. Pudding, better. Chocolate Bread Pudding, yes, Yes, YES! You'll have a hard time turning down seconds when this bad boy comes out of the oven. Just be sure to pause long enough to breathe!

1 tablespoon vegan butter, plus more for greasing baking dish

10 slices (10 ounces) vegan cinnamon-raisin bread or thick-sliced white bread

1 ½ cups unsweetened almond milk

4 ounces semisweet vegan chocolate (about ½ cup)

½ cup ice-cold unsweetened almond milk

2 tablespoons VeganEgg powder

½ cup evaporated cane sugar

¼ teaspoon sea salt

¼ teaspoon ground cinnamon

½ teaspoon vanilla extract

1 tablespoon powdered sugar, for topping

**01**  Preheat oven to 350°F.

**02**  Lightly grease 9-inch baking dish with vegan butter. Set aside.

**03**  Place slices of bread on a flat baking sheet and toast bread in oven until lightly crisped, about 5 minutes.

**04**  Heat medium saucepan over medium-low heat. To saucepan add 1 ½ cups almond milk, chocolate, and tablespoon vegan butter. Cook about 5 minutes to melt chocolate, stirring occasionally. Remove from heat and transfer to a large bowl or flat dish to cool until about room temperature. Set aside.

**05**  Whisk ½ cup ice-cold almond milk with VeganEgg powder until smooth and slightly thickened. Set aside.

**06**  Tear bread into large pieces and scatter evenly in greased baking dish.

**07**  Add VeganEgg mixture to bowl with cooled chocolate mixture. Add sugar, sea salt, cinnamon, and vanilla. Whisk until uniform. Pour over bread.

*(Directions continued on next page)*

*(Continued from previous page)*

**08** Bake until pudding has puffed slightly and is firm, about 40 minutes. Cool at least 10 minutes, and dust with powdered sugar just before serving.

# Whole Wheat Chocolate Cupcakes with Whipped Cream Cheese Filling

## BY SPORK FOODS

**YIELDS:** 1 Dozen  **DIFFICULTY:** Moderate
**PREP TIME:** 20 Minutes  **COOK TIME:** 24-26 Minutes

### TOOLS YOU'LL NEED

What's the difference between a cupcake and a muffin? ... Give up? The answer is the technicalities of the mixing process (though isn't the real answer frosting?), so although these cupcakes are made like muffins, their whipped cream cheese filling and frosting makes them cupcakes in our book.

### Cupcake Ingredients

1 cup unsweetened almond milk

1 teaspoon apple cider vinegar

1 ½ cup unbleached all-purpose flour

½ cup whole wheat pastry flour

¼ teaspoon ground cinnamon

¼ teaspoon cardamom

1 ½ teaspoons aluminum-free baking powder

½ teaspoon sea salt

1 cup evaporated cane sugar

¼ cup unsweetened cocoa powder

2 tablespoons VeganEgg powder

¼ cup ice-cold water

2 teaspoons vanilla extract

⅓ cup neutral-tasting oil (safflower)

¼ cup vegan chocolate chips

01  Preheat oven to 350°F. Line cupcake pan with liners and spray with non-stick spray if liners are not waxed.

02  In a measuring cup, add milk and apple cider vinegar and let curdle about 2 minutes.

03  In a medium bowl, add flours, cinnamon, cardamom, baking powder, sea salt, sugar and cocoa powder. Whisk until uniform.

04  In a separate bowl, combine VeganEgg powder and ice-cold water. Whisk until smooth and slightly thickened. Add curdled almond milk, vanilla extract, and oil. Whisk until uniform. Add into dry ingredients and whisk until just blended. Fold in chocolate chips.

05  Fill liners ¾ high. Bake 24-26 minutes or until toothpick comes out clean.

06  To create filling, in a bowl of a stand mixer whisk vegan butter and cream cheese until uniform.

*(Ingredients & Directions continued on next page)*

*(Continued from previous page)*

**Cream Cheese Filling Ingredients**

2 tablespoons vegan butter

3 rounded tablespoons Follow
Your Heart Cream Cheese

3 cups powdered sugar

½ teaspoon vanilla extract

Dash sea salt

Add powdered sugar, vanilla extract, and sea salt.
Whisk until fluffy.

**07** To fill cupcakes, pipe cream cheese filling into
center of cupcake and then frost top to seal in
area where filling comes out of the top.

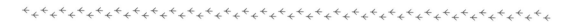

# Spiced Banana Bread with Toasted Hazelnuts

## BY SPORK FOODS

**YIELDS:** 1 Loaf  **DIFFICULTY:** Moderate
**PREP TIME:** 10-15 Minutes  **COOK TIME:** 65-70 Minutes

### TOOLS YOU'LL NEED

When we were kids, nothing said fall like the smell of fresh banana bread baking in the kitchen when we came home from school. This light and fluffy spiced banana bread is topped with toasted hazelnuts for a scrumptious, nutty crunch. And, if you like your bread extra nutty, toss in a few extra hazelnuts into the batter before you bake it.

½ cup whole wheat pastry flour

1 ¼ cups unbleached all-purpose flour

½ teaspoon ground cinnamon

¼ teaspoon ground nutmeg

2 teaspoons baking powder

½ teaspoon sea salt

¾ cup evaporated cane sugar

¾ cup ice-cold unsweetened almond milk

2 level tablespoons VeganEgg powder

⅓ cup neutral-tasting oil (safflower)

1 teaspoon vanilla extract

1 teaspoon apple cider vinegar

2 ripe bananas, mashed

2 tablespoons hazelnut pieces, for topping

**01**  Preheat oven to 350°F. Grease loaf pan (9 x 5).

**02**  In a medium bowl, whisk flours, cinnamon, nutmeg, baking powder, sea salt and sugar.

**03**  In a separate bowl, whisk ice-cold almond milk with VeganEgg powder until smooth and slightly thickened, about 1 minute. Add to dry ingredients with oil, vanilla, and apple cider vinegar. Whisk until uniform.

**04**  Fold in mashed banana and mix until uniform, being careful not to overmix. Mixture will be thicker than traditional cake batter.

**05**  Add batter to greased loaf pan. Top with a sprinkling of hazelnuts.

**06**  Bake for 65-70 minutes or until toothpick comes out clean in center. Leave in pan for 10-15 minutes, then transfer to cooling rack and cool before slicing.

# *Vanilla Bean Custard*

## BY SPORK FOODS

**SERVES:** 4  **DIFFICULTY:** Moderate
**PREP TIME:** 10 Minutes  **COOK TIME:** 10 Minutes

### TOOLS YOU'LL NEED

A single whole vanilla bean is a potent little gem! With this recipe, simply slice it lengthwise to let loose the magic seeds inside and they will come to life as they simmer and steep. Keep an eye on this one because you want to keep the mixture moving so it doesn't start to set up before you're ready. (Gluten-Free)

¼ cup VeganEgg powder

1 cup ice-cold unsweetened almond milk

½ cup raw cashews

1 ½ cups unsweetened almond milk

1 vanilla bean, split lengthwise

½ cup evaporated cane sugar

¼ teaspoon sea salt

¼ teaspoon ground cinnamon

2 teaspoons vanilla extract

**01** In a small bowl, add VeganEgg powder and 1 cup ice-cold almond milk. Whisk until smooth and slightly thickened, about 1 minute. Set aside.

**02** In high-powered blender or food processor, combine cashews and 1 ½ cups almond milk. Blend until smooth. Don't clean blender or food processor. Add cashew mixture to a 4-quart pot.

**03** Add split vanilla bean, evaporated cane sugar, sea salt, and cinnamon to pot. While stirring, heat to a simmer and cook at a simmer for about 2-3 minutes, continuing to stir constantly.

**04** Add VeganEgg mixture to pot and cook over medium-low heat, whisking constantly for 3 minutes. Remove from heat and whisk in vanilla extract. Remove vanilla bean.

**05** Place cooked mixture in same blender or food processor. Blend until smooth and aerated. You may need to scrape the sides, making sure to not catch spatula on blade. Divide evenly among 4 ramekins or cocottes. Let cool at room temperature for about 15-20 minutes.

*(Directions continued on next page)*

*(Continued from previous page)*

**06** Place in refrigerator and chill for at least 1 hour before serving.

**07** Serve in ramekins with fresh fruit or run a small knife along edge of each ramekin or cocotte, then invert onto small serving plates.

Baby Turkeys © 2017 Farm Sanctuary, Inc.

Luke @ Woodstock Farm Sanctuary

Johnny @ Woodstock Farm Sanctuary

Pamela © 2017 Farm Sanctuary, Inc.

# Farm Sanctuaries

## COMPASSION FOR ALL

One of our missions at Follow Your Heart is to contribute to the well-being and betterment of the Earth and all its inhabitants. For us, that includes those that have skin, fur, feathers, scales or any number of legs. Our revolutionary VeganEgg provides a sustainable, humane alternative to eggs, allowing you to more easily enjoy a plant-based diet. To the farm sanctuaries around the US, we want to thank you by dedicating this book to you for your continued work for all of Earth's inhabitants.

Animal sanctuaries are home to neglected, abused, abandoned, and rescued farm and even wild animals including chickens, cows, pigs, horses, goats, sheep, turkeys, and more. These rescued animals, each with their own story, are given a second chance once they've made their way to safe and loving sanctuaries. They spend their days free from the neglect and cruelty of factory farming, in a peaceful environment where they are cherished and appreciated as members of the farm family.

In their new homes, these fortunate animals are given the freedom, necessary veterinary care, and individual attention they need to be happy and flourish. Their days are spent basking in the sun, digging in the dirt, enjoying acres of wide-open land, and playing freely with their fellow animal friends of many diverse species.

Since most farm sanctuaries are nonprofits that run on donations, community support is key for their survival. This is our chance to get involved. Sanctuaries often host community events and welcome visitors and volunteers to tour the farms, interact, and help with the animals. These are great opportunities to hear the stories of the rescued, what kind of help they're receiving, and what we can do to make a difference. We get to connect with these farm animals that most of us are typically so distant from and discover that each has an individual personality. Seeing these animals thrive in a peaceful environment allows us to see first-hand the benefits of living plant-based.

Follow Your Heart has the utmost gratitude towards all animal sanctuaries and the kind hearts that keep them up and running. We know that operating an animal sanctuary takes not only drive and compassion, but also a great deal of time, money, and skill. If you operate or volunteer at an animal sanctuary in your area, please contact us for partnership inquiries at info@followyourheart.com.

Have you hugged a chicken today? Thanks to farm and animal sanctuaries across the US and world, you very well could have and tomorrow you probably can!

Atticus and Moby @ Woodstock Farm Sanctuary

# Following Our Hearts

For over 40 years, Follow Your Heart has been committed to the same ideals and values we started with in 1970. From our humble beginnings as a small market and café in Southern California, we have expanded our passion for great-tasting, plant-based foods into the company that you know and love today. We believe that all people deserve access to healthy food, that all living things deserve compassion, and that we have a responsibility to be good stewards of the Earth.

Earth Island is our very own manufacturing facility that produces the Follow Your Heart products that are shipped across the US and around the world. Since we moved here in 2003, every jar of Vegenaise that has hit shelves and landed in your refrigerator was mixed in our kitchen just behind these doors. Every single carton of VeganEgg was loaded on a truck just to the right of this picture and sent across the country and across oceans to the many retailers that carry our products.

Our buildings are topped with solar panels and our commitment to sustainability has recently led Earth Island to become Zero Waste certified. We're the first food manufacturer in Southern California to be certified Zero Waste and we couldn't be prouder!

That passion that began in 1970 continues today with everyone at our original Follow Your Heart market and restaurant, our Earth Island manufacturing facility, and our Rising Hearts gluten-free bakery. We thank every employee who has walked through our companies' doors for their hard work, dedication, and what they've contributed to making Follow Your Heart, Earth Island, and Rising Hearts what they are today. As our family continues to grow, we are glad to have you, the reader, as part of our journey and look forward to many more years of creating innovative and impactful products for a better world.

Earth Garden at Earth Island

# 40 Years of Flavor

## OUR FAMILY OF PRODUCTS

Over the last four decades, we have created a diverse array of delicious, innovative products which have been enjoyed by folks around the world. In this cookbook, you'll find many Follow Your Heart products used in recipes. We would like everyone to be able to get their hands on all of our products at their local market. If you need help finding them, we invite you to check out our online store locator, where you can pick a product or a particular flavor, and search locally. (The flavors listed below are available at time of publishing.)

### Vegenaise

Since we first created it in the early 1970s, Vegenaise has grown to become the most-loved, egg-free sandwich spread among vegans, vegetarians, and anyone looking for a healthier, more sustainable option to mayonnaise. Our customers agree that it's Better than Mayo®!

Original - Soy Free - Grapeseed Oil - Reduced Fat - Organic - Roasted Garlic - Pesto - Chipotle - Sriracha - Barbecue - Horseradish Sauce - Tartar Sauce

### Vegan Cheese

Continuing to pioneer new vegan products, in 2003, we launched the first-ever melting vegan cheese! We introduced Vegan Gourmet Cheese to an overwhelmingly positive response and since then, we've decided to never stop innovating for the dairy-free consumer. Our current line-up of dairy alternatives includes the original blocks (now made with organic ingredients), our new Soy-Free Shreds (which are convenient and deliciously creamy) and our even newer Soy-Free Slices and Blocks (which are so amazing, our fans are eating them right out of the package and calling them a game changer!) Dairy-free Cream Cheese and Sour Cream? Yep, we've got them too.

Mozzarella - American - Provolone - Garden Herb - Smoked Gouda - Pepper Jack - Cheddar - Parmesan - Fiesta Blend - Pizzeria Blend - Monterey Jack - Nacho - Cream Cheese - Sour Cream

### Salad Dressings

Salads from our Follow Your Heart Market and Café became locally famous in part because of the lusciously creamy dressings that we created for them. We continue that tradition today with our hand-crafted line of Salad Dressings and Sauces, made fresh and kept refrigerated to maintain that homemade taste to the last drop.

High Omega Vegan Ranch - High Omega Vegan Bleu Cheese - Organic Vegan Caesar - Organic Balsamic Vinaigrette - Vegan Thousand Island - Vegan Honey Mustard - Vegan Creamy Garlic - Vegan Lemon Herb - Organic Miso Ginger - Low Fat Balsamic Vinaigrette - Original Balsamic Vinaigrette - Organic Italian Vinaigrette - Spicy Balsamic Barbecue - Reduced Fat Vegan Ranch - Reduced Fat Southwestern Vegan Ranch

### VeganEgg

For over a decade now, we have narrowed our sights on an egg substitute that not only replaces eggs for baking and emulsifying, but also acts and tastes like real eggs when scrambled and cooked in omelets and frittatas. The first 100% plant-based whole egg replacer is finally here.

VeganEgg

### Gluten-Free Bakery

With our passion for wholesome foods and a love for baking, we expanded our offering to include hand-crafted delicious, nutritious and immensely satisfying gluten-free breads and tortillas.

Brioche Bread - Millet Bread - Oat Bread - Classic Tortillas - Flax & Chia Seed Tortillas

And there's many MANY more to come...

# A VeganEgg is Hatched

When we set out to create a plant-based egg we knew it wasn't going to be easy, but we were up to the challenge. For years, Bob Goldberg, our founder and head of our Research & Development, had dreamed of creating a fully functional egg alternative. We'd spent years developing delicious products that avoided using eggs because of their environmental and ethical impact and knew it was time to turn our focus from avoiding eggs to replacing them. The prospect of creating an "egg" that scrambled in a pan, worked in baking, and performed in a multitude of recipes was something that we knew was possible, we just had to get there.

Enter Dr. Erin Keys. The addition of Dr. Keys to our team and the technical experience she brought with her led us to new breakthroughs in our recipe development. We explored new ingredients and processes, and through many months of trial and error, office tastings, and a lot of failed scrambled eggs later, we created VeganEgg. It made great breads and omelettes, we mastered the vegan quiche, and, of course, the classic scramble. We then set to work as quickly as we could to bring this amazing product to your local store shelves.

All of the ingredients in VeganEgg are plant-based, gluten-free, dairy-free, and non-GMO. In addition to functioning like eggs, VeganEgg is a good source of dietary fiber and calcium, and compared to eggs, has less than half the fat and no cholesterol. Plus, the carton is compostable, recyclable, and made with recycled materials. We're proud that VeganEgg is a revolutionary step toward a more sustainable and more humane world.

100 VEGANEGGS CAN BE MADE
WITH THE SAME WATER USED TO
PRODUCE ONE CHICKEN EGG

# Why Plant-Based?

For many of you, this may all be old news, but for those of you who are new to a plant-based diet, here are some reasons why people across the US and the world are eating vegan at a higher rate than ever before.

## Animals

One of the more common reasons for becoming vegan is a love for animals of all species, as evidenced in this cookbook with so many people dedicating their work to farm sanctuaries. There are now alternatives to traditionally animal-based foods, such as non-dairy milks, cheeses, meats, and more. Saving animals is easier than it's ever been when it comes to the foods we have available.

## Health

Plants and plant-based foods are rich in protein, calcium, iron, and a wide range of vitamins and minerals. In addition to the nutrients they contain, vegan foods are often lower in saturated fats and cholesterol and tend to be high in fiber. Research has shown that these features of a balanced plant-based diet help reduce heart disease, obesity, and diabetes.

## Environment

Plant-based is a greener way to live because plant-based foods are generally produced with less water, less land, a lower carbon footprint, and plus, they're a more humane way of eating. By not furthering the negative impacts of factory farming such as polluted water runoff and deforestation for producing animal feed and grazing, going vegan is a powerful way to protect the environment.

Spork Foods

Colleen Patrick-Goudreau

Brian Patton

Olivia Roszkowski for Naturally, Danny Seo

Carolyn Scott-Hamilton

Acooba Scott

Chris Petrellese and Jasmine Briones

# Our Heartfelt Gratitude

## TO OUR CONTRIBUTORS

Los Angeles-based **Spork Foods** is a gourmet vegan food company owned and operated by sisters Jenny Engel and Heather Bell. They offer live vegan cooking classes in Los Angeles (www.sporkfoods.com) as well as teaching all over the world, reaching over 10,000 people a year. They are the authors of the Spork-Fed cookbook and Vegan 101, with a foreword by fellow fans Emily and Zooey Deschanel. Heather and Jenny are also chef ambassadors for Follow Your Heart. @sporkfoods

**Jasmine Briones**, also known as Sweet Simple Vegan, is a plant-based nutritionist, photographer and lifestyle blogger. Jasmine shares recipes and lifestyle tips inspiring others towards conscious, healthy, and positive choices. @sweetsimplevegan

**Chris Petrellese**, foodie and photographer behind the Instagram account and blog Conscious Chris. Inspired by mindful and compassionate living, Chris is sharing his vegan journey through photos, recipes, and lifestyle tips. @consciouschris

For **Acooba Scott**, cooking has always been about creativity and love. Growing up (and learning to cook) in a Third World country, she had to be extra creative, as even some basic ingredients such as wheat flour or cooking oil would often be in short supply. Vegan cooking has given Acooba the opportunity to be innovative, as well as express love, not only for herself and her own body, but also for her loved ones, for the animals that would otherwise be harmed, for the local environment, and for the entire planet. For over 25 years, Acooba has been fully engaged in designing and building a healthy, plant-based lifestyle with her husband and their four children. She loves sharing the tips and tools she uses to make vegan living accessible, nourishing, fun and deliciously sustainable! @acoobascott

**Brian L. Patton** a.k.a. The Sexy Vegan is a vegan chef, cookbook author, popular social media personality, and founder of 99Publishing.com, where he creates expertly crafted, single-recipe cookbooks. He credits Follow Your Heart's products with easing his transition to veganism a decade ago, as well as with adding to the excitement and creativity in his cooking today. Brian may or may not also snort lines of the VeganEgg for breakfast. @thesexyvegan

**Carolyn Scott-Hamilton** a.k.a. The Healthy Voyager, is the creator and host of The Healthy Voyager web series, website, and overall brand. An award-winning healthy, special diet and green living and travel expert, holistic nutritionist, plant-based vegan chef, best-selling cookbook author, media spokesperson, sought-after speaker, consultant and television personality, Carolyn Scott-Hamilton is a respected figure in the world of healthy lifestyle and travel as well as special diet cooking and nutrition. The Healthy Voyager aims to help people live well, one veggie at a time! @healthyvoyager

**Naturally, Danny Seo** has long been a fan of Follow Your Heart and their family of plant-based products. If you look in founding Editor-in-Chief Danny Seo's kitchen, you're sure to find it fully stocked with Vegenaise, VeganEgg and a few slices of their dairy-free cheese slices.

**Colleen Patrick-Goudreau** is forever changing how we talk about, think about, and treat other animals. She is a bestselling author of seven books, acclaimed speaker, and creator and host of the award-winning podcast, "Food for Thought." Colleen is a regular contributor to National Public Radio (KQED) and has appeared on national and regional TV programs, including the Food Network, CBS, PBS, and FOX. Interviews with her have been featured on NPR, Huffington Post, U.S. News and World Report, The Chicago Tribune, The Miami Times, Pacifica Radio, Rodale News, and in countless publications, blogs, and podcasts. She is a monthly guest on Good Day Sacramento. @joyfulvegan

*(Continued on next page)*

Chef Tal Ronnen    Thug Kitchen

Chef Robin Swallow    Gabrielle St. Claire

Jackie Poles Ran

Rashi Bhatnagar    Erin and Jeff Wysocarski

# Our Heartfelt Gratitude
## TO OUR CONTRIBUTORS

**Gabrielle St. Claire** a.k.a. EatDrinkShrink is the founder and creator of EatDrinkShrink.com. She is an NYC-based holistic nutritionist who holds a BS and MS in Clinical Nutrition. She works in vegan recipe development, privately teaches yoga, and is a future vegan cookbook author. @eat.drink.shrink

**Erin Wysocarski** a.k.a. Olives for Dinner is the creator and recipe developer at OlivesforDinner.com, a globally-inspired vegan blog, while her husband, **Jeff**, handles all the photography. "We love Follow Your Heart's VeganEgg for its innovation, versatility and authentic taste and texture!" @olivesfordinner

**Jackie Poles Ran** started her food career back in 1986 as a vegan teenager working in the grocery department at Follow Your Heart. From there she went on to college earning her Bachelor's Degree in Nutrition and her Master's Degree in Food Science. Jackie worked in the food industry for years before finding her way back home to Earth Island as their Director of Product Development. Jackie enjoys inspiring others to make compassionate food choices by feeding them tasty vegan food and sharing her latest restaurant finds. She believes that if food is good, people will eat it and if it's all plant-based, then it's a win-win for everyone! @beinvegan

**Rashi Bhatnagar** has always been very passionate about food and the science behind it and this passion brought her to working with the R&D team at Earth Island/Follow Your Heart. She is currently pursuing a food science degree and works on many of the upcoming products that are set to launch for Follow Your Heart. "I love that VeganEgg is such a versatile ingredient and I enjoy experimenting with it in my kitchen!"

**Robin Swallow** is the owner and Executive Chef of Manna Restaurant in London and former Executive Chef of Follow Your Heart in Canoga Park, California. With over 25 years of experience in cooking vegetarian and vegan food she currently enjoys spending her time teaching vegan cooking classes here in Los Angeles and in London. @robinswallow

An internationally renowned chef, best-selling author, and the 2013 VegNews Person of the Year, **Chef Tal Ronnen** has pioneered an entirely new cuisine that pairs a sophisticated sensibility with an emphasis on plant-based foods and ingredients. Ronnen's signature style of cooking has made him a favorite among celebrities and foodies. He is perhaps best known to the public at large for helping open Chrissie Hynde's VegiTerranean restaurant in Akron, OH; catering the wedding of Ellen DeGeneres and Portia de Rossi; and creating the menu for Oprah Winfrey during her 21-day vegan cleanse. The release of his newest book, Crossroads (Artisan Books), has been featured in Food & Wine magazine, The New York Times, USA Today, and is an International Association of Culinary Professionals (IACP), Cookbook Award Finalist. @crossroadskitchen

**Thug Kitchen** blew up the Internet back in 2012, when Michelle Davis and Matt Holloway began blogging and, after winning Saveur's Best New Food Blog of 2013, the team decided to make it official by writing a book. All three of their books, Thug Kitchen: Eat Like You Give a F*ck, Thug Kitchen: Party Grub, and Thug Kitchen 101: Fast as F*ck, became instant New York Times best sellers and now with their books translated into over 7 different languages and counting, Thug Kitchen is a certified global phenomenon. @thugkitchen

# Acknowledgements

Thank you Bob Goldberg and Paul Lewin, our founders and leaders, for your endless inspiration and guidance. Jenny Engel and Heather Bell of Spork Foods, the gratitude that we have for your help on this cookbook is unmeasurable. Dr. Erin Keys for your commitment to making our beloved VeganEgg a reality and for your achievements on the many more products we have in the pipeline. Sara Farwell and Cristine Kasha for taking this cookbook idea and making it a beautiful reality. The entire Earth Island R&D department for the dedication and creativity you bring to our food innovations. Colleen Holland and the VegNews staff for your support of Follow Your Heart over the years. Gene Baur and farm sanctuaries everywhere for your compassion and the work you do for animals every day. A big thank you to our recipe and photo contributors for your talent and ingenuity. Katie Franklin, Oscar Mendoza, Austin Allen, and Sheena DeBellis for your additional contributions to this book. Matt Dunaj, Laura Sklov, Rory Richmond, and the entire Earth Island office for your patience as we took over the tiny breakroom kitchen and for tasting all of our recipes, and last but not least, the employees of Earth Island that make our Follow Your Heart products so that people everywhere can enjoy them at home!

# *Index*

## A

Apples
   Prosecco-Battered Apple Fritters 90

## B

Baking with VeganEgg 07

Bell Pepper
   Rancho Chilaquiles 34
   Classic Fried Rice with Scrambled VeganEgg 68

Black Beans
   Chipotle Breakfast Burrito 26
   Breakfast Tacos with Creamy Tomatillo Sauce 44

Black Pepper 04

Bread
   Spinach, "Ham," & Provolone Cheese Strata 22
   Classic French Toast 30
   Chocolate Bread Pudding 100

Breakfast Frittata Pie 18

Breakfast Tacos with Creamy Tomatillo Sauce 44

Brioche Bread 123
*(See also Follow Your Heart Brioche Bread)*

## C

Carrots
   Classic Fried Rice with Scrambled VeganEgg 68

Challah 92

Cheddar 123
*(See also Follow Your Heart Cheddar Cheese)*

Chipotle Breakfast Burrito 26

Chipotle Vegenaise
   Chipotle Breakfast Burrito 26
   Breakfast Tacos with Creamy Tomatillo Sauce 46

Chive & Cheese Scrambled VeganEggs 14

Chocolate Bread Pudding 100

Chocolate Chips
   Rich Chocolate Brownies 84
   Soft-Batch Chocolate Chip Cookies 88

Whole Wheat Chocolate Cupcakes with Whipped Cream Cheese Filling 104

Classic French Toast 30

Classic Fried Rice with Scrambled VeganEgg 68

Coconut Creamer
   Quiche Florentine 28

Cream Cheese 121
*(See also Follow Your Heart Cream Cheese)*
   Whole Wheat Chocolate Cupcakes with Whipped Cream Cheese Filling 104

Creamy Tomatillo Sauce 44

## D

Dairy-Free Milk 05

## E

Earth Island 119

Evaporated Cane Sugar 05

## F

Follow Your Heart American
   "Sausage" & VeganEgg Biscuit Sandwich 42
   "Ham," VeganEgg, & Cheese Puffs 50

Follow Your Heart Brioche Bread
   Spinach, "Ham," & Provolone Cheese Strata 22

Follow Your Heart Cheddar Cheese
   Mashed Potato Waffles 52

Follow Your Heart Cream Cheese
   Whole Wheat Chocolate Cupcakes with Whipped Cream Cheese Filling 104

Follow Your Heart Gluten-Free Brioche
   Classic French Toast 30

Follow Your Heart Gluten-Free Tortillas 123
   Chipotle Breakfast Burrito 26

Follow Your Heart Mozzarella
   Breakfast Frittata Pie 18

Follow Your Heart Parmesan
   Spinach, "Ham," & Provolone Cheese Strata 22
   Lentil Meatballs 70

Follow Your Heart Provolone
    Chive & Cheese Scrambled VeganEggs 14
    Spinach, "Ham," & Provolone Cheese Strata 22
    Quiche Florentine 28

Follow Your Heart Sour Cream
    Mashed Potato Waffles 52

Follow Your Heart Vegenaise
    Scrambled VeganEgg Salad 66

Fresh Homemade Pasta 60

## G

Garlic
    Breakfast Frittata Pie 18
    Rancho Chilaquiles 32
    Summertime Tomato & Basil Pasta 64
    Lentil Meatballs 70
    Smoky Eggplant Burgers 74
    Vegan Matzo Ball Soup 78

Gluten-Free 125
    The Perfect Scramble 10
    Chive & Cheese Scrambled VeganEggs 14
    Breakfast Frittata Pie 18
    Spinach, "Ham," & Provolone Cheese Strata 22
    Chipotle Breakfast Burrito 26
    Quiche Florentine 28
    Classic French Toast 30
    Rancho Chilaquiles 32
    Breakfast Tacos with Creamy Tomatillo Sauce 44
    Spanish Omelette (Tortilla Española) 56
    Scrambled VeganEgg Salad 66
    Classic Fried Rice with Scrambled VeganEgg 68
    Smoky Eggplant Burgers 74
    Vanilla Bean Custard 110

Green Peas
    Classic Fried Rice with Scrambled VeganEgg 68

## H

"Ham," VeganEgg, & Cheese Puffs 50

Hash Browns
    Breakfast Frittata Pie 18
    Chipotle Breakfast Burrito 26

## J

Jalapeño
    Rancho Chilaquiles 32

## L

Lentil Meatballs 70

## M

Mashed Potato Waffles 52

Measuring VeganEgg 07

Mixing VeganEgg 07

Mushrooms
    Breakfast Frittata Pie 18

## N

Neutral-Tasting Oil 04
(See also Safflower Oil)

## O

Onion
    Breakfast Frittata Pie 18
    Spinach, "Ham," & Provolone Cheese Strata 22
    Rancho Chilaquiles 32
    Breakfast Tacos with Creamy Tomatillo Sauce 44
    Spanish Omelette (Tortilla Española) 56
    Scrambled VeganEgg Salad 6
    Classic Fried Rice with Scrambled VeganEgg 68
    Lentil Meatballs 70
    Smoky Eggplant Burgers 74
    Vegan Matzo Ball Soup 78

Orange Cranberry Baked Donuts 96

## P

Parmesan 123
(See also Follow Your Heart Parmesan)

Pecans
    Pecan Waffles 16
    Pumpkin French Toast Casserole 36

Pecan Waffles 16

Pico de Gallo
> Chipotle Breakfast Burrito 26
> Rancho Chilaquiles 32

Pie Crust
> Quiche Florentine 28

Plant-Based 115, 125, 129

Potatoes
> Mashed Potato Waffles 52
> Spanish Omelette (Tortilla Española) 56

Prosecco-Battered Apple Fritters 90

Provolone 123
*(See also Follow Your Heart Provolone)*

Pumpkin French Toast Casserole 36

## Q

Quiche Florentine 28

## R

Rancho Chilaquiles 32

Rich Chocolate Brownies 84

Rising Hearts 119

## S

Safflower Oil 04

Salsa
> Breakfast Tacos with Creamy Tomatillo Sauce 44

"Sausage" & VeganEgg Biscuit Sandwich 40

Scrambled VeganEgg Salad 66

Sea Salt 04

Shallots
> Quiche Florentine 28

Smoky Eggplant Burgers 74

Soft-Batch Chocolate Chip Cookies 88

Sour Cream 123
*(See also Follow Your Heart Sour Cream)*
> Mashed Potato Waffles 52

Spanish Omelette (Tortilla Española) 56

Spiced Banana Bread with Toasted Hazelnuts 108

Spinach
> Breakfast Frittata Pie 18
> Spinach, "Ham," & Provolone Cheese Strata 22
> Quiche Florentine 28
> Rancho Chilaquiles 32

Spinach, "Ham," & Provolone Cheese Strata 22

Storing VeganEgg 07

Summertime Tomato & Basil Pasta 64

## T

The Perfect Scramble 10

Tomatoes
> Breakfast Frittata Pie 18
> Rancho Chilaquiles 32
> Summertime Tomato & Basil Pasta 64
> Smoky Eggplant Burgers 74

Tortillas
> Rancho Chilaquiles 32

## V

Vanilla Bean Custard 110

Vegan Bacon Bits
> Breakfast Frittata Pie 18

Vegan Breakfast Sausage
> "Sausage" & VeganEgg Biscuit Sandwich 40

Vegan Butter 04

Vegan Ham
> Spinach, "Ham," & Provolone Cheese Strata 22
> "Ham," VeganEgg, & Cheese Puffs 50

Vegan Matzo Ball Soup 78

Vegenaise 119, 123
> Scrambled VeganEgg Salad 66
> Smoky Eggplant Burgers 74

## W

Whole Wheat Chocolate Cupcakes with Whipped Cream Cheese Filling 104

## Z

Zero Waste 119